American Indians
in Colorado

Cover design by Bonnie Donato, this Arapaho eagle design appears on many American Indian arts and crafts.

American Indians in Colorado

J. DONALD HUGHES

PRUETT **P** PUBLISHING COMPANY
Boulder, Colorado

First Edition

2 3 4 5 6 7 8 9

Printed in the United States of America

Library of Congress Cataloging in Publication Data

Hughes, Johnson Donald, 1932-
    American Indians in Colorado.

    (Colorado ethnic history series ; no. 1)
    Bibliography: p.
    Includes index.
    SUMMARY: Traces the history of Colorado's Indians
from the early bison hunters and the rise of the Plains
culture to the continuing attempts to maintain Indian
identity in the American society.
    1. Indians of North America--Colorado. 2. Ute
Indians. [1. Indians of North America--Colorado.
2. Ute Indians] I. Title. II. Series.
E78.C6H83   978.8′004′97   76-54523
ISBN 0-87108-206-3

University of Denver
Department of History
Colorado Ethnic History Series
No. 1

iv

Introduction

Since I have spent some time in Colorado working with the various bands of Ute Indians which comprise the Southern Utes and the Ute Mountain Utes, this book held a particular fascination for me. One of the significant impressions was the importance of the area now known as Colorado to so many tribes of Indians and groups of Indian people.

This well-written book brings into lively focus the continuing change which seemed to affect the area and its original peoples, so that a reader will feel almost a part of the changing scene as the history of the area unfolds. It would have been an unforgettable experience if one's lifetime could have spanned the years of colorful and exciting history, but I believe one can still capture the flow of events from the book enough to arouse both interest and enthusiasm for learning about the American Indians in Colorado.

It is true that the Ute Indian people in Southwest Colorado are living a more sedentary life, contrasted with their early history of high mobility, but, in their own way, they are still making history. A visit to the modern day Ute Indian communities impresses one with the feeling that things are still going on and events are in the making. These are described well for those readers who will not have the good fortune of becoming acquainted with these fine, friendly people.

Other Indian tribes are represented in some of the cosmopolitan areas, such as Denver, whose past is intertwined with the historical events of Colorado, some of which is not to the credit of the "Strangers Who Came," but nevertheless comprise their history. These descendants of the various Indian tribal groups are making a contribution to the development and growth of the State, but they are at the same time not forgetting and not letting anyone else forget their glorious traditions.

I have been fortunate on two counts; one for having had the opportunity to read the book and the other for having had the experience of living and working with these wonderful people — *American Indians in Colorado.* I would like to share this good fortune by recommending the reading of this book for knowledge and for pleasure.

Robert L. Bennett
U.S. Commissioner of Indian Affairs, 1966–69
Member, Oneida Indian Tribe

Contents

To Peter and Melissa

Indian People

"The war-whoop re-echoes no longer,
The Indian's only a name, . . ."

says the official Colorado state song, adopted in 1915.[1] At that
time, it seemed to many people that Indians were about to
disappear. The author of the song, Arthur John Fynn, was
fair-minded and friendly to Indians, but he believed in the old
idea of the "vanishing Red Man." Whatever people used to
think, the Indians have not vanished, and today it is clear that
they are here to stay.

The number of Indian people in Colorado is increasing
rapidly; in fact, their population is growing much faster than
that of the state as a whole. The 1960 census reported about
4,300 Indians in Colorado, and the figure increased to about
8,800 in 1970. Although census figures in regard to Indians
are not exact, they do show a rapid growth that is real. Indians
are increasing because families tend to be large, because with
improving health more Indian children survive, and because
many Indians from other states are moving to Colorado.

Indian people take an active part in the life of Colorado.
They have an importance and influence far beyond their numbers. Only two Indian reservations are in the state, both in
the southwestern section near the cities of Durango and Cortez.
The Ute Mountain Indian reservation occupies the extreme
southwest corner of Colorado and extends a little into New
Mexico. The tribal capital is at Towaòc, Colorado. Extending
eastward from that reservation along the southern boundary
of the state is the Southern Ute Indian reservation, with
headquarters at Ignacio, Colorado. Together, these two Ute
reservations include about 2,000 Indian residents. But most
Indians in Colorado do not live on reservations. About four
times as many live in the metropolitan area, including Denver
and Boulder, and in other cities around the state, such as
Colorado Springs and Durango. They live side by side with

1

people of other backgrounds. They work at jobs of every kind, including teaching, heading U.S. government agencies, and serving in the state legislature. However, unemployment is a serious problem for many Indian people. They live in homes similar to those of their neighbors. They dress like others of their own age and sex, except at Indian gatherings, celebrations, or shows. Then they may put on their traditional clothing, which is admired by many people for its artistic decorations, patterns, and colors.

American Indians are living people in the present. They also have a great heritage from the past which has given much and continues to give to themselves, to Colorado, America, and to the world. Their ancestors were the first inhabitants of this continent, the first to know the mountains and plains, the lakes and rivers, of this beautiful land. They were the first to give them names. They learned the ways of the animals and treated them with respect even when they hunted them. They found out the uses of plants and later shared that knowledge with others. Their skill in crafts led them to make beautiful objects. They sang during work and play, and in worshipping the great power found in nature. Their wise elders knew all these things and taught them to the young people.

Today, Indian culture is still active. Many Indians are learning skills to keep traditional arts and crafts alive, and their weaving, leatherwork, beadwork and quillwork, basketry, silverwork, and other jewelry crafts are in great demand. But Indian artists have also adapted their heritage to modern modes of expression. They paint pictures in traditional and contemporary styles, write poetry, stories and novels, write and produce their own drama, choreograph their own dances, and compose and play music that has an Indian sound, though the instruments may be modern and the style "classical" or "rock." Today, many Indians as well as non-Indians are convinced that Indian cultures and philosophies have much to offer.

All Americans need to know more about the Indian heritage. Too often other people's ideas about Indians come only from the movies and television. Even books are not always helpful in giving a good, balanced picture of what Indians are really like, and what they have done.

One of the most important things to remember about Indians is that they are not all the same. Indian tribes are as different from each other as the English are from the Italians, or the French from the Russians. In some ways the differences are greater, in other ways they are less. Take languages, for example. There is no such thing as *"the* Indian language." When English colonists first landed on the east coast, more than 400 different languages, many unrelated, were being spoken by American Indians. Many of these are still spoken. Ute is a living language in Colorado. The Navajo language, spoken by more people in the United States than any other American Indian language, is the mother tongue of many who live in Denver. Indians from different tribes are often different in body build and facial characteristics. More important, different tribes have different traditions which affect how they perceive life and how they act.

Indians of many different tribes live in Colorado. In early times the Pueblos, Utes, Shoshones, Cheyennes, Arapahoes, Apaches, Comanches, and Navajos, along with other tribes, lived here. Still others visited and hunted. Today, in addition to the Utes, Colorado is home to Indians from dozens of tribes and from every part of the United States, including Alaska. The tribes with the greatest numbers in Denver are the Navajo and Sioux (Dakota), with members of at least forty other tribes represented. Due to this great variety, it is hard to generalize. Statements that begin with "The Indian is . . ." or "The Indian thinks . . ." are always suspect. There never has been a "typical Indian," and probably never will be. The reader is warned to be cautious with all statements about Indians in general, including the ones in this book. It is up to each Indian to decide for himself or herself what it is like to be an Indian. Certainly no Indian from another tribe, and especially no White "expert," has the right to make that decision for someone else.

Who are the Indian people? In early times many tribes called themselves "the people," and they decided who was part of the tribe, and who was not. To some extent, this is still true. But in United States history, different ways have determined who is an Indian and who is not. Three of the most important are (1) ancestry or "blood," (2) legal definitions, and (3) culture; that is, ways of life and the experience of being treated as an Indian by family and society at large.

Ancestry can be expressed as a fraction. Many Indians are full-blooded descendants of one tribe. Others have parents, grandparents, or more distant ancestors who are from other tribes, or who are non-Indians. For example, if your father were Indian and your mother White, your "blood-quantum" would be one half. Then, if you married a White person and had children, their "blood-quantum" would be one fourth. Many federal laws, and many Indian tribes, regard one fourth as the minimum "blood-quantum" requirement to be officially recognized as an Indian, but there are many exceptions. Of course, ancestry has a lot to do with physical appearance. A full-blooded Indian will certainly show his or her Indian blood. But an Indian with a one-fourth "blood-quantum" might have blond hair and blue eyes, and might not be readily recognized as an Indian. It is important to remember that such a person may be fully Indian before the law, may have been brought up as an Indian, and may consider himself or herself to be completely Indian.

Since 1924, and in some cases prior to that date, all native-born American Indians have been recognized as full citizens of the United States and of the states of their residence. Indians have all the privileges and duties of citizenship. They are guaranteed the right to vote, are required to pay certain taxes, and are not individually regarded as "wards of the government." In 1968 the Indian Civil Rights Act was specifically extended to all American Indian citizens. But Indians do have a special relationship to the United States government, because many laws apply only to them. More than 100 years ago, many treaties between the federal government and various Indian tribes stipulated that Indians would give up huge areas of land, receiving from the government either payment or services such as education and health care. Although the treaties have not always been honored, they are still part of United States law unless changed by Congress.

The government has had to define an "Indian," so that they can determine who is eligible for special services and subject to special laws. You are an Indian, according to United States law, if your name is on a "tribal roll," or list of members kept by a recognized tribe. There are some problems with this definition, because only about half of all the people who consider themselves to be Indians are listed on the tribal rolls. The federal courts seem to be deciding that some people who are not on the rolls, including many Indians who live in cities, may also legally be Indians and therefore entitled to some services. This is not just a technicality. Indian education has been considered a major responsibility of the federal government for four generations. Nevertheless, on the average, Indians leave school much earlier than any other group of Americans. Their health, which is generally the responsibility of the federal government, is in the worst state of any group in the nation.

Culture is the best way to decide who is an Indian, but it is not an easy yardstick to apply. You are an Indian if you live in a genuine Indian way, if you think of yourself as an Indian, and are regarded by others as an Indian. The individual raised by an Indian family and treated by society as an Indian will be Indian. This means living as an Indian in the modern world, not necessarily adhering to someone's idea of what Indian life was like before any contact with White people. An Indian is not less Indian because he or she drives a car or masters English spelling. For several generations, Indians have culturally defined themselves in relation to Whites and others. They have not lived in isolation. On the other hand, many Indians are striving not to lose their Indian identity. They do not want to give up what is essentially Indian about them. They do not want to become just like everyone else; "an apple," red on the outside and white on the inside. Indians have not and will not become White people.

For close to a century, the ultimate aim of United States Indian policy has been "assimilation," which means making Indians into White people, or as much like White people as possible. This was done by taking Indian children away from their parents and educating them in schools far from their homes, sometimes not even allowing visits. Indian languages and religions were forbidden, and their use or practice was severely punished. Indians were forced to cut their hair, wear White clothes, and learn White jobs, usually the least desirable ones. They were made to feel like strangers in their own land. But they resisted, and in spite of the pressure to "assimilate," they have remained Indians. They can take pride in their survival.

Not all these things are being done at present. But Indian people, many of whom come from rural reservation areas where the old traditions are not dead, usually find the ways of urban Americans hard to understand at first. Generally, Indians come from large extended families where cooperation and care for one another are the rules. They tend to feel that life in the big cities is cold, selfish, and lonely. Indian children were taught to be considerate and helpful, and often do not like to compete

5

with others and "get ahead." Sometimes Indian children do not like to raise their hands in class, because this might embarrass others who do not know the answer. They love to play games like basketball, but may not want to keep score. Indians often do not value time as White city dwellers do. Indian meetings tend to start when everyone is there and ready, and they end when everyone has said everything he or she wants to say. Agreement is generally reached by common consent, not by rigid and divisive majority votes. No one is forced to agree. On the other hand, Indian values have long encouraged them to accept the world as it is, and to suffer without speaking out or complaining. White people have been accustomed to changing the world to suit themselves whenever possible. All these differences between Indian and White ways of thinking and doing have made it very hard for most Indians to get along in a society in which rules are made by urban Whites.

At the same time, Indians usually have not felt any common interest with other minority groups in American society. European ethnic groups like the Irish or Italians seem just like other Whites to Indians. Black people have had a different history, and their ways of approaching their problems seem to be different from the Indian way. To Indians, Blacks seem to share many White values. The Spanish-speaking people, even with their White European heritage, are closer to Indian culture in some ways. Many also have some Indian background, which can be strong and important to them. But the American Southwest, of which Colorado is historically a part, has been the scene of conflict, land controversy, and cultural distinction between the Indians and Spanish-speaking people since long before the United States conquest. Indians find that they can cooperate with people of Spanish or Mexican background in working for some goals, but not for others.

Indians are different from other people for several important reasons. Indians cherish a particularly rich cultural background in relation to their own tribes. As the original inhabitants of America, they feel a special affection for the land and a reverence for nature. Even those who live in cities have real attachments to their tribal land, and often return to visit family and friends. Indians have a special legal relationship to the federal government, unlike any other group of people in America. United States law has always placed the major responsibility for Indian policy in Washington rather than in the states or local communities. It should be clear to the reader that these distinctions are the result of a different historical experience. Indian history has been different from the history of any other people. By understanding their own history, Indian people can learn to understand themselves. And by studying Indian history, other people can come to understand Indian people.

The purpose of this book is to briefly outline the Indian history of what is now the state of Colorado. During the centennial of Colorado statehood and the bicentennial of United States independence, citizens are turning to their history with renewed interest. Indians have always played an important role in the history of Colorado. Beginning with the hunters of huge Ice Age animals and rising to early heights with the great cliff cities of Mesa Verde, their saga continues through the development of plains and mountain cultures. Later chapters begin with the arrival of White explorers and settlers, continue through the bitter struggle against encroachment and domination, and culminate in the long attempt, not yet over, to maintain cultural identity within a nation dominated by another society. In tracing this history, we will try to keep a wide view, noticing national events that affected Colorado. We will regard as Colorado Indians all Indians, regardless of tribe, who came to live in Colorado. We will look not only at "Indian country" and the reservations, but also at the cities. We will regard as history not just the storied deeds of the romantic past, but also the living actions of those who are making history today.

The Ancient Ones

American Indians were the first people to live in Colorado. In school we are usually taught that Columbus discovered America and that the Spanish were the first explorers of the area we now call Colorado. But White Europeans were actually late comers. The earliest discoverers and explorers of this continent were the ancestors of the Indians, and they arrived many thousands of years ago.

Just how long ago is not certain, because we must suppose that all the evidence has not yet been found. The most reliable indication to archaeologists that people were in Colorado in very early times would be to find their bones. Human skeletal material has been found and dated back to almost 8000 B.C. But earlier remains of campfires, bones of large mammals, and chipped stone projectile points indicate that human beings were in Colorado at least 12,000 years ago.

Most scientists now agree that the ancestors of the American Indians crossed the Bering Straits from Asia to Alaska. Physical type between the various American Indian groups varies considerably, but Indians seem most closely related to the Asiatic or Mongoloid peoples. Like them, they tend to have straight black hair and dark eyes. But in some ways, particularly in blood type frequencies, American Indians and East Asiatics are quite distinct, and some scientists consider American Indians (Red) to be the fourth major group of the human race, along with Negroids (Black), Caucasoids (White), and Mongoloids (Yellow). A possible conclusion is that the ancestors of the American Indian left Asia so long ago that certain specific characteristics of the modern people of East Asia had not yet developed. The Indians adapted to the varied environmental conditions of their new homes in North and South America. This idea finds support in the fact that the northernmost groups of American Indians, like the Eskimo, are most like the East Asiatic peoples in appearance. The Eskimo were possibly the last people to arrive from Asia; they still remain in contact with their neighbors across the Bering Straits.

Scientists do not agree on when the migrations to the New World took place. New methods of dating, in addition to the radiocarbon method, have been used to claim great age for various human remains in Canada, the United States, and Mexico. The dates range from 10,000 B.C. to almost 50,000 B.C., that is, perhaps even beyond the last ice age to a relatively ice-free period between the glacial advances. Many archaeologists are skeptical about the earlier dates and wait for better evidence. Others predict that evidence of human occupation in America will eventually be found dating to between 50,000 and 100,000 B.C. There is even an isolated and controversial date from Mexico of 200,000 B.C. which cannot be accepted without further support. All these dates, though they may seem like a long time ago when measured against our own lifetimes, are comparatively recent when compared with the finds of human or prehuman remains in the Eastern Hemisphere. In Africa, dates of two to four *million* years B.C. have recently been assigned. Mankind evidently did not originate in the New World, but came here from the Old.

It seems certain that American Indian ancestors were in Colorado when the northern lands were in the grip of the most recent great ice age, the Wisconsin glaciation. The climate was colder than it is now. The great ice masses did not cover Colorado, although huge glaciers did fill the higher valleys of the Rocky Mountains. In fact, it is thought that the Ice Age was partially interrupted by relatively warmer periods, and that at times one could have walked all the way from Alaska to Colorado down the eastern flank of the Rockies without crossing glaciers or ice fields.

In those times, Colorado was the habitat of many large mammals that later became extinct, such as mammoths, camels, horses, giant bison much larger than the buffalo of today, and giant ground sloths. They lived along with the other, more familiar animals that managed to survive, like deer, foxes, wolves, rabbits, and pronghorn antelope. The first people we know about in Colorado were skilled hunters of the largest mammals.

Around 9200 B.C., a group of Colorado hunters killed at least a dozen mammoths, perhaps by driving them over a cliff and then attacking them with boulders and stone-tipped spears or javelins. At Dent, near Greeley, Colorado, huge elephant bones were found with the large, deftly fashioned, channeled projectile points called "Clovis points." These weapons were apparently designed specifically to kill mammoths. When American elephants became extinct about 9000 B.C., the hunters turned to other game, especially the giant bison, and changed the style of their hard stone projectile points to the famous "Folsom" type. These are shorter (about two inches long as compared with four to five inches for the larger Clovis points), grooved, leaf-shaped points, with earlike projections at the base. The Folsom site, named after a nearby town in New Mexico, was found in 1926, along with the bones of ancient bison, by a Black cowboy named George McJunkin. The site was carefully studied by scientists from the Denver Museum of Natural History. Jesse Dade Figgins, leader of the team, found one point embedded between two bison ribs, and thus definitely established that extinct animals had been hunted by human beings in America.

The largest and most important Folsom site is on the Lindenmeier ranch, north of Fort Collins, Colorado. At the site a hunters' camp and kills of bison and camel were radiocarbon dated at 8820 B.C., and a Folsom point was found embedded in a bison vertebra. Tools found there include not only the distinctive points in two sizes, but also knives, scrapers, gravers, and choppers. Bone was worked into awls, knives, and beads. The Folsom people evidently occupied much of Colorado, since the points have been found in many places around the state. Other Folsom sites in Colorado include a camp near Greeley and bison kills near the Great Sand Dunes in the San Luis Valley.

The bison hunting tradition continued on the plains for thousands of years, but conditions changed and new projectile point shapes were knapped from stone. The giant *Bison antiquus* was replaced about 7000 B.C. by the somewhat smaller *Bison occidentalis* and the even smaller *Bison bison*, which survived to become the "buffalo" of recent times. The climate was becoming warmer and drier, and the vegetation less abundant. This may help to explain why the larger mammals became extinct. Some paleontologists believe that the hunters were responsible for the disappearance of the animals they hunted, by being wasteful in game drives, setting grass and forest fires, and driving large herds over the cliffs. This seems unlikely, because Indians have always been careful hunters, killing only as much game as was actually needed

11

and using almost every part of the slain animals for food, clothing, tools, and utensils. Indians had a practical working knowledge of what would be called ecology today, and they knew that if they killed too many animals, famine would occur in succeeding years. When White people arrived in America, the plains were still covered with millions of buffalo. It was only a deliberate policy of slaughter with firearms that enabled White men to wipe out the wildlife heritage of the Indians in a few decades.

The methods of early bison hunters were revealed in fascinating detail by an archaeological excavation in 1967 at a kill site near Kit Carson, Colorado, under the direction of Joe Ben Wheat of the University of Colorado Museum. Around 6500 B.C. a large group of hunters surrounded on three sides a herd of nearly 200 buffalo of the species *Bison occidentalis*. Driving them into a steep gulch about twelve feet deep, the hunters used their spears to keep the bison headed in the right direction. The dead animals were carefully and systematically butchered, with all the similar parts such as legs and skulls placed together. Only thirteen of the animals were not butchered. The skins would have been used for clothing, blankets, or shelter, and the excess meat that was not eaten fresh was no doubt preserved by drying. Dr. Wheat estimated that the band of hunters, including their families, numbered at least 150.

As early as 7000 B.C., another tradition existed west of the plains in the mountains, foothills, and the increasingly dry plateau areas of the Colorado River drainage. These people, who belonged to what has been called the Desert culture, did not depend greatly on big game hunting. They foraged for a variety of foods, including wild plants and medium-sized or small game such as deer, bear, rabbits, and squirrels. They hunted larger animals like the giant ground sloth when they could be found. They used grinding stones called metates and manos for the wild seeds they gathered. Baskets, woven sandals, and fiber nets are known from before 6000 B.C. Our most complete knowledge of the Desert culture comes from caves in Utah and Nevada, but many sites are known in Colorado, including some in the Dinosaur and Colorado National Monument areas near Grand Junction.

On the high plains, Indians continued to hunt for thousands of years, but no longer depended so much on big game. A hot, dry period from 4000 to 3000 B.C. made vegetation more sparse and animals less plentiful. Along with bison, hunters sought deer, antelope, birds, and reptiles, and supplemented their diets with wild plants. They still made projectile points in a variety of shapes and used stones to grind seeds. As time passed, influences reached the plains from the Desert culture to the west and the Woodland culture to the east. Small notched or stemmed points show that the bow and arrow were adopted as the main hunting weapons. Pottery marked with cord impressions, like that made in the eastern woodlands, appeared in Colorado before 1000 A.D., but was not widely used. While Indians farther east were adopting agriculture and village life, and building burial mounds, those living in Colorado retained the older hunting and gathering mode of life called the Plains Archaic tradition.

Indians of Desert culture background in southwestern Colorado began to cultivate maize (corn) before 1 A.D., and agriculture altered their way of life. Corn came to Colorado from regions to the south, where it had been known for a long time. As long ago as 6000 B.C., Indians of central Mexico had taken the wild ancestor of corn, with its tiny cobs and few kernels individually protected by pods, and had begun the long process of planting and selection that eventually produced the marvelously productive plant of modern times. Small ears of corn, dated at about 3000 B.C., have been found in southern New Mexico. They were a form of popcorn, as shown by the popped kernels found in the ancient caves. Accompanying corn on its slow movement north came squash—another plant early domesticated by the Indians—with its many forms including the pumpkin. The seeds of sunflower, a native North American plant, were eaten by Basketmakers, but we do not know if the plants were cultivated.

The Colorado Indians who first began to plant corn and squash are called Basketmakers because of the great variety of well-made, beautifully decorated baskets found among their remains. The first Basketmakers were not very different from their predecessors of the Desert culture. Like them, they used metates and manos to grind plant seeds, now including the dried kernels of corn. Agriculture did not displace the older practices of hunting and foraging. They continued to hunt wild animals with throwing sticks and spears aided by spear throwers, or atlatls, long sticks notched at the upper end for the base of the spear. The atlatl effectively lengthened the hunter's arm and gave added leverage to speed the projectile's flight and to give it added force on impact. Basketmaking was inherited from the Desert culture, along with the fashioning of mats, netting, and sandals. Food was cooked by placing hot rocks in baskets.

The Colorado Basketmakers settled where they could plant and cultivate their crops; movements from place to place were not as easy for agricultural people as they were for their foraging ancestors. They tilled the earth with simple, sharpened digging sticks. Their dwellings are called pithouses because they consisted of an excavated foundation with a roof supported by poles and covered with bark and earth. Entrance was through a covered passage from the side or through the hatchway at the top, which also served as an exit for smoke. Some of the earliest known Basketmaker houses were found near Durango, Colorado, in the drainage of the San Juan River and its northern tributaries. Pithouses near the Animas River have tree-ring dates between 46 and 330 A.D. The Basket-makers' preferred sheltered locations under overhanging sandstone cliffs as homesites. These shelters have preserved many of the objects used in the peoples' daily lives, so we can say more about them as compared to other early Indians.

They wore robes of fur strips or deerskin, and flat woven sandals of yucca or Indian hemp. The women wore aprons of juniper bark or yucca. Fine woven belts or sashes have been found. Men wore their hair long, but women used their hair in weaving, and thus necessarily kept it short. They were fond of ornaments such as necklaces and ear pendants made of stone, shell traded from the Pacific Ocean, bone, seeds, and feathers. Their baskets were both beautiful and functional, serving a variety of purposes as utensils. Some were woven tightly enough to carry water. The Basketmakers kept dogs of different breeds and possibly used them in hunting. It is likely that dogs were brought to America by early people who came over from Asia.

After the fifth century A.D., the Basketmakers were generally living in established villages of well-developed pithouses. They learned to make pottery from people farther south, and copied the functional shapes of baskets and gourds in their gray ware, to which they sometimes added decorations in black paint. New varieties of corn appeared in their fields, and they began to grow beans. These two crops, with squash, make up the three mainstays of native North American agriculture. Turkey bones and feathers have been found, indicating that the Basketmakers may have domesticated that useful bird. They made carefully ground, polished stone axes and hammers with grooves for the attachment of handles. Probably during this period they learned to use an efficient new weapon, the bow and arrow.

That the Basketmakers had rich religious rituals is clear from the evidence of petroglyphs and clay figurines which show human beings, animals, and kachina-like figures. They smoked native tobacco in tubular "pipes," probably only on ceremonial occasions, and played music on six-hole flutes like those still used in the Hopi flute dance. Their medicine men assembled curative plants, minerals, and other sacred objects in special bundles, and made prayer sticks or medicine arrows adorned with feathers as offerings. The care with which they buried their dead, including grave offerings, indicates that they believed in some kind of life after death.

Niman kachina dance at Shungopovi, a Hopi village. Photo by Adam Clark Vroman, 1901. *Courtesy Smithsonian Institution National Anthropological Archives, Bureau of American Ethnology Collection.*

Around 700 A.D., major changes occurred in the Basket-maker way of life, causing archaeologists to apply a different name—Pueblo—to the cultural tradition. "Pueblo," a Spanish word meaning "town," refers to the fact that their rectangular houses were now built above ground, first of poles and adobe mud, and later of good stone masonry. Today, archaeologists often refer to the Basketmaker-ancient Pueblo cultural tradition by using the single term "Anasazi," a Navajo word which means "Ancient Ones." Actually, the Basketmakers were the ancestors of the ancient Pueblo Indians, and the ancient Pueblo Indians were the ancestors of the modern Hopis of Arizona and the Zunis and other Pueblo Indians of New Mexico. There was no break in the tradition. But the existence of a variety of different languages among modern Pueblos hints at a fascinating history of movements of people and cultural enrichment. Although the story cannot be told in detail, it is an element in many of the traditional oral histories which still survive among Pueblo Indians.

The Pueblo people at first abandoned the cliff shelters to build their new villages in the open. Although they constructed square or rectangular living rooms on the surface, they continued to make their ceremonial rooms, or kivas, underground in the circular form of the traditional pithouse of their Basket-maker ancestors. The growing size of Pueblo communities apparently made larger kivas necessary for everyone to participate in indoor ceremonials. Great kivas, much larger than those of separate clans, first made their appearance in Colorado. However, they reached their greatest development at a later time in Aztec Ruins and Chaco Canyon, New Mexico, where they are from forty to sixty feet in diameter.

Along with a new style of architecture, the ancient Pueblo Indians adopted a new way of caring for their infants. Instead of the soft, padded carrying basket used by the Basketmakers, the Pueblos wrapped their babies on a rigid—but not uncomfortable—cradle board, which gradually formed the soft, growing bones of the skull into a rounder shape, more flat in the back.

As Pueblo agriculture continued to develop, extensive works were built to control the flow of water and prevent erosion. Floodwater irrigation enabled Pueblo farmers to raise crops intensively in a dry land.

Cotton appeared as a domestic plant in the early Pueblo period. Its origin is not exactly known, which presents interesting grounds for historical speculation. Wild cotton is known in both the Old World and the New. However, cultivated cotton in the New World shows genetic evidence of having come not from New World wild cotton alone, as would be expected, but from a cross between New World and Old World cottons. No one suggests that Old World cotton could have been brought over the Bering Straits. However, occasional contacts across the Pacific, or possibly even the Atlantic, are possible, though none before the Viking visit of about 1000 A.D. can be securely demonstrated at present. Could cotton have arrived in ancient or medieval times on a venturesome ship from Asia? Whatever the answer, there is no doubt that Pueblo Indians learned to weave fine textiles from cotton, and apparently the new fiber made it unnecessary for women to cut their hair for use in weaving. Pueblo women began to arrange their long hair in two ties, one on each side of the head, and this remained the traditional arrangement. Cotton continued as a Pueblo crop, and today Pueblo weavers still use cotton, along with wool.

The art of fine basketry never died out among the Pueblos, but it was replaced for most uses by increasingly well-made pottery in a wide variety of shapes. Pueblo pottery was characterized by bold black designs painted on a white or grayish background. It was made from long coils of clay, placed in circular or spiral fashion one above the other, and then smoothed out or adorned with indentations. The potter's wheel was unknown in ancient America.

In the mid-eleventh century A.D., the Pueblo Indians entered a period of cultural flourishing known as the Classic, or Great Pueblo period. At this time huge dwellings were built containing hundreds of living and storage rooms, complete with many kivas and tall square or circular towers. Many structures took on a distinctly defensive appearance, with thick walls and watchtowers located in spots that would be difficult to attack. Within a relatively short time, some of the outlying settlements were abandoned, their inhabitants presumably having moved into larger centers. Archaeologists have found evidence of the movement of other tribes through Colorado during this period. It is quite probable that Athapascan-speaking people (the ancestors of the Apaches and Navajos) from what is now Canada were making their presence felt.

No ancient Pueblo ruins are more famous than the cliff dwellings at Mesa Verde National Park, Colorado. Thousands

Cliff Palace, Mesa Verde, Colorado. *Courtesy State Historical Society of Colorado.*

of visitors see Cliff Palace, Spruce Tree House, Square Tower House, Balcony House, Long House, and others every year. These represent the culmination of ancient Pueblo culture in Colorado. The people practiced intensive agriculture, using stone hoes, on the flat mesa tops and in other favorable spots. Their pottery and weaving were of the finest. They painted their bodies and the walls of their dwellings in rich natural colors. The influences of the great civilizations then flourishing in Mexico traveled north with trade. Macaw feathers, and even the live birds, were prized, and copper bells tinkled among a people who had never before known the use of metal. The process of mosaic inlay with turquoise, jet, shell, and other materials was known in Mexico long before it was practiced as an art among the Pueblos. Certain art motifs seem to be related to those found farther south. Certain elements of Pueblo mythology and ceremony, perhaps including the snake dance, may also be related to the southern cultures. The ancient Pueblos were not "southwesterners"; they were on the northern edge of the widespread area of the Mesoamerican civilization.

The Pueblo Indians had a rich religious life centering around nature, the progress of the seasons, and crop growing. The petroglyphs, paintings, and other objects found in the ruins lead us to believe that much of their way of life, including religion, survives today among modern Pueblo Indians—who

18

are noted for their faithfulness to the practices of their ancestors. The kivas at Mesa Verde are circular, almost totally underground (even when this meant excavation in virtually solid rock), with log crib roofs covered with earth. Since no great kivas are found in the cliff dwellings, we assume that each of the several kivas in a pueblo belonged to a different clan, and that large public ceremonies were held in an open area, or plaza. Each kiva had a fireplace with a smoke aperture above, through which a ladder provided the only entrance. Fresh air entered through a vertical shaft at one side, and was prevented from blowing into the fire by a stone deflector. On the opposite side of the fire, a covered hole in the floor symbolically represented the sipapu. This was the entrance to the underworld, the place from which it was believed the people had originally climbed up onto the surface of the present world.

By 1300 A.D., the Pueblo Indians suddenly and mysteriously abandoned Colorado. They appear to have packed all the belongings they cared to carry, and moved south to other Pueblo settlements in Arizona and New Mexico, where their descendants still live. There are few signs of violence, although the presence of hostile tribes might have contributed to their decision to leave. The record of climate preserved in the rings of trees indicates that a long series of dry years occurred between A.D. 1276 and 1299, the period when the Mesa Verde pueblos were abandoned. Some scientists suggest that the climate change was accompanied by severely increased erosion which prevented the people from using even the reduced amount of rainfall.

Although the Pueblo Indians left Colorado, they flourished in their new homes, building even larger cities, developing more colorful and delicate pottery, and keeping all their arts alive. The old idea that the Pueblos entered a "regressive phase" or decline after 1300 A.D. has been thoroughly disproved. Rather, they continued to develop right to the time of the Spanish conquest in the late sixteenth century, and in many ways continued to maintain their own culture in the face of European influence. Today, many Pueblo Indians live in Colorado, although no Pueblo towns exist in the state. Most of them live in Denver and its surrounding communities but maintain strong personal and family ties with the particular Pueblo towns in New Mexico or Arizona in which they find their roots.

Pueblo influences reached beyond the Four Corners country into northwestern Colorado, the home of Indians belonging to what archaeologists have called the Fremont culture. Although Fremont people lived during the Classic Pueblo period, they made their homes in small villages of pithouses and sometimes surface dwellings more like those of the earlier Pueblo people. They did not build kivas. Small storage structures are numerous. They raised corn, beans, and squash, and continued to gather wild plants and to hunt mountain sheep, rabbits, deer, elk, and other animals with the bow and arrow. Unlike the Pueblo Indians, they did not have grooved axes, did not grow cotton, and lacked turkeys. They made good baskets, and their pottery was gray, tempered with crushed rock, and sometimes decorated with black paint. They ground their corn on shovel-shaped metates with an extra depression at the closed end. Instead of sandals, they wore moccasins of mountain sheep hide. They made clay figurines, many representing females wearing an apronlike garment, and decorated rock surfaces with some of the most well-executed petroglyphs and pictographs known in America.

The Fremont people may have been Indians of the Desert culture who adopted agriculture and other Pueblo traits, but retained much of their earlier way of life. Like the Pueblo culture, the Fremont culture disappeared from Colorado. Perhaps the people left the area, or perhaps under the pressures of the great drought and enemies on the move, they reverted to the hunting and foraging ways which had already assured survival in a difficult environment for thousands of years. It is quite probable that these resourceful people were the ancestors of the Utes and other people of Shoshonean languages who have had a central role in Colorado history, and about whom we will have much more to say.

Not much has been said in this chapter about the Rocky Mountains in the central part of Colorado. This is not because early Indians did not live there, but because so few archaeological investigations have been conducted in the mountains. Evidence of Indian occupation has been noticed in the highest areas above timberline. Presumably, Indians from both east and west of the mountains made seasonal hunting trips into the high country. Some hunters may have stayed in the mountain region all the time. Their way of life was no doubt closest to that of the Desert culture.

Indian Tribes of Colorado

Several important Indian tribes have lived in Colorado in the past few centuries. The Utes, Apaches, Navajos, Shoshones, Comanches, Kiowas, Kiowa-Apaches, Arapahoes, and Cheyennes made their homes in the land that became Colorado, and the Pueblos sometimes returned to the north from their nearby towns. Indians of other tribes, such as the Pawnee and Sioux, entered Colorado from time to time while hunting, warring, or trading. Too many books on state history leave the reader with the impression that the only true Colorado tribes were the Utes, Arapahoes, and Cheyennes. These three tribes occupied most of the area when White Americans began to trap, mine, and settle, but others, too, have lived among the mountains and plains and hold important places in the history of Colorado.

Each tribe regarded itself as distinct from all others. Until very recently, no feeling of "Indian" unity existed among them, although two or three tribes might be friendly and offer to help each other. A tribe usually named itself "the people," "our people," "the real people," or "the human beings." Other tribes and White people were regarded as foreigners; they might be treated with hospitality, respect, friendship, or enmity, but except in rare instances of individuals being adopted into the tribe, they remained outsiders.

Tribes differed in language, traditions, ways of life, and historical experience. There also were similarities, but it is difficult to generalize about Colorado Indians. Each tribe must be seen as a separate group of people, different from any other. It should also be noted that the basic unit of organization or government was usually not the whole tribe, but a smaller unit, or band. Only rarely did a single chief lead an entire tribe. Most often, bands composed of a few families chose their own chiefs from among family leaders. In emergencies, bands might cooperate with each other. But generally speaking, Indian tribes were not strongly unified under chiefs, like small European kingdoms. That incorrect idea was made up by Europeans who wanted to deal with the Indians.

Anthropologists classify Indian tribes by cultural area. Within each area exist similarities in ways of life. Colorado is the meeting point of three cultural areas: the Great Basin, the Southwest, and the Plains. Indians here were part of, or influenced by, one or more of the three cultural traditions.

The Utes and Shoshones are usually classed with the Great Basin tribes. The Desert culture was located in the Great Basin, and the ways of life of the people there resembled the traditions of the Desert culture. However, both the Utes and Shoshones were deeply influenced by the Plains culture, so that they are sometimes considered marginal Plains Indians. The Utes also shared many traits with the southwestern tribes. The southwestern tribes include the Pueblo Indians, whose way of life fairly typifies the Southwest culture, the Navajos, and to some extent the Jicarilla Apaches, who also have many Plains attributes. All other Colorado tribes were Plains Indians, and the influence of Plains culture affected the entire area. It is important, then, to get some idea of what Plains Indians were like before we begin to talk about the history of individual tribes.

The Plains Indian has become the image of the "typical Indian" in the minds of non-Indian Americans and Europeans. Through books and motion pictures, through radio and television, the world has become familiar with the nomadic Indian mounted on his horse, brandishing his rifle, with his feathered warbonnet trailing in the wind, riding out from his circle of tepees to hunt the buffalo or to attack the wagon train or cavalry column. It is hard to connect this stereotype with any tribe of Indians that actually existed, but if any Indians were ever like that, they were those who lived on the Great Plains in the nineteenth century. It is misleading to think that all Indians fit such an oversimplified, exaggerated picture. Plains Indians have a much richer and varied history than that distorted image would suggest.

Plains Indian tribes lived in the huge, almost treeless grasslands which stretch from Canada to Texas, and from the Rocky Mountains to the states that lie immediately west of the Mississippi River. We tend to think of them as horse-riding Indians who hunted buffalo with rifles, but both the horse and rifle came to the Plains Indians in fairly recent times—the horse from both the Spanish people and Indian tribes in New Mexico, and the rifle from the French and British traders to the east. The Plains culture itself is far older and predates contact with the European Whites.

The first Spanish explorer to enter the Great Plains, Coronado, found Plains Indians in New Mexico and Kansas (and perhaps even the southeastern corner of Colorado) in 1540. Spanish accounts describe the Plains Indians as they were before the horse and rifle. They depended on the buffalo, planted no crops, and used buffalo products for everything. Their shelters were large tepees covered with skillfully tanned hides. They wore clothes and moccasins sewn from the hide with buffalo sinew; they made tools from the bones and often used buffalo chips as fuel for their fires, since there was so little wood on the Great Plains. After a buffalo kill, the Plains Indians cut much of the meat into strips. By drying it in the sun, they produced "jerky" that could later be boiled and eaten. When they followed the buffalo, they packed their belongings on the backs of their large dogs, or on a "travois" of dragging tepee poles pulled by a dog. (Later, the horse would also pull the travois.)

Many Plains Indians were excellent with the bow and arrow. They traded with the Pueblo Indians, exchanging hides and meat for maize and cotton cloth, and could overcome language barriers by using the sophisticated language of hand

Cheyenne women collecting roots of the yampa plant. *Courtesy Museum of the American Indian, Heye Foundation.*

signs. Thus, the pattern of life in the ecological area of the Great Plains had been created before White contact. The horse and rifle added speed of movement and killing power to Plains culture and encouraged other changes, but the basic pattern was adapted to the new factors with surprising ease.

The Plains tribes came from different stocks and places of origin, and they spoke a wide variety of languages. But in other ways they resembled each other. They were all primarily hunters of the buffalo and other large animals such as elk, deer, and antelope. Most Plains tribes moved with the hunt, taking their tepees with them to favored locations. However, some of the more easterly tribes lived in established villages of earth lodges and supplemented their meat diet with maize, beans, and squash raised in the river bottoms. In earlier times, semiagricultural Plains Indians lived in eastern Colorado.

Men and women all worked, doing different tasks. The men hunted and fought, and the women gathered or planted vegetable foods. Men cut poles for the tepees, but women put up the tepees and dressed the skin coverings. Both men and women made artistic decorations and participated in ceremonies. Clothes were sewn from softened, dressed skins with or without fur, adorned with fringes and designs of dyed porcupine quills. Men wore shirts, leggings, moccasins, and deerskin aprons or breechcloths. In cold weather they wrapped themselves in buffalo robes, and in hot weather, or when hunting or fighting, they would go without shirts or leggings. Nothing was worn on the head, except during ceremonies when the famous warbonnet, buffalo-horn cap, or other elaborate headgear were donned. Women wore a one-piece, long dress which stretched from chin to ankles. It covered the upper arms, but had no sleeves, and was often decorated with elk's teeth, paintings, or porcupine quillwork. Their moccasins were worn below knee-high leggings.

The fine crafts of Plains Indians were leatherworking, skin painting, quillwork, dyeing, and some specialized forms of wood carving (such as cradleboards and saddles). They did little weaving or basket making, and their pottery, if made at all, was undecorated and simple. People on the move do not like to carry heavy pots.

Plains Indian warfare was distinguished by such an elaborate code of conduct that it has been called a form of chivalry. It was one of the major ways for men to gain status, the others being generosity in gift giving and medicine power won through self discipline and visions. The warrior's main purpose was to demonstrate his courage by touching the enemy with a stick (a "coup") without being harmed himself, or by being the first to touch an enemy after he was killed. The war leader wanted to direct a successful raid, capturing horses and prisoners and perhaps killing enemy warriors, without losing any of his own men. The battles were often highly stylized, more like medieval European tournaments than modern wars, the women of opposing groups sometimes gathering on the surrounding high ground to observe and cheer their champions. Weapons were bows and arrows, stone-tipped clubs, spears, and decorated shields of buffalo hide. Pitched battles were very rare, and wars were not usually fought to capture territory; rather, they were fought to revenge traditional enemies. Enemy tribes occasionally made peace, and the role of peacemaker within a tribe was highly honored.

Each tribe had membership societies, both for men and for women. Some societies were religious, while others, such as the "Dog Soldiers" of the Cheyenne, were military, often performing a police function.

Plains Indian government was essentially democratic. All members of the tribe or band had an opportunity to rise to leadership if their abilities so merited. There was no hereditary class of chiefs; titles were won through demonstrated courage in battle and visions. All responsible persons had some voice in running the affairs of the group, and although men held most positions of honor, women were also known to exercise great wisdom and power. Frequently the household, including the children and the tepee, were the women's property. Most tribes lived in divided locations for most of the year, so effective leadership was exercised by able individuals in the bands.

Indians everywhere placed a high value on speaking ability, and the arts of the orator and storyteller were prized. Traditional stories of heroes, the creation, and the old days when things were different were told on long winter nights.

Indians never separated religion from the rest of life. It was a part of every activity, and the individual and the tribe tried to keep in balance with the universe at all times. An individual might seek power in a vision quest, practicing personal disciplines of purification and self-denial culminating in a vigil when voices might be heard, wonderful sights seen, and special songs learned. Such a person might afterwards be able to heal others or lead ceremonies.

Tribal ceremonials could be very elaborate, with prayers and songs accompanied by drums, rattles, and rasps. (Flutes were also known, but were usually used by serenading lovers.) Sacred objects, especially the tobacco pipe, were brought forth and sacred bundles were opened. Dances were sometimes a part of ceremonials, but unlike tribes elsewhere, the Plains Indians did not often wear masks.

The Sun Dance was the most important ceremonial of almost all Plains tribes. Certain persons would dance for several days in an enclosure, facing a sacred pole which might carry special objects such as a buffalo robe or skull, or a doll. The search for power and the good of the tribe are central in the Sun Dance; a few tribes practiced special ascetic disciplines. They would pierce their chests and insert wooden pegs attached by leather thongs to the central pole. The thongs gradually tore themselves free during the course of the dance. The idea was to give part of oneself—of one's own body—and to test one's courage. The Sun Dance, with or without the piercing, has had a great revival in more recent times.

Now let us look at each of the Colorado tribes, exploring how they fit into the Plains, Great Basin, or Southwest cultural patterns, and examining their early history before the White man became an important factor in their lives. The Utes should come first because they have a longer continuous history in Colorado than any other tribe and because their traditional lands occupied the greatest portion of the state. The Utes have played a central role in Colorado's history and are the only Indians who now hold reservations within its borders.

Scholars do not generally agree as to when the Utes entered Colorado, or from where they came, but the Utes themselves will tell you they have lived here since the beginning. There is good reason to agree; it is quite probable that they are the living descendants of the Desert culture, the Fremont people, and perhaps the Basketmakers, and if so, their residence in Colorado dates back 10,000 years or more.

The Utes speak one of the Shoshonean languages, quite similar to the tongues of the Shoshones, Comanches, Bannocks, and Paiutes. These groups are related to the Great Basin tradition, and the Utes recognize them as relatives in varying degrees. More distantly related languages are spoken by the Hopis, some of the California Indians, and even the Aztecs of Mexico. This whole language family is called Uto-Aztecan.

Utes occupied all of the mountainous lands in Colorado, from the Yampa River in the northwest to the San Juan River in the southwest, from the slopes of the front range in the east to the present western border; in all, well over half of the state. They hunted buffalo as far out onto the plains as the shadows of the Rockies stretch at sunset. Their homelands also included central and eastern Utah and parts of northern New Mexico.

Their way of life was hunting and gathering; only rarely did they plant a crop of maize or beans. Thus, they spent the warmer months moving as family groups through their customary hunting territories, often high in the mountains. In winter they moved with the game to the southern parts of their range, or into the lower valleys. For a period in the spring they settled with other members of their own band, a major section of the tribe which had its own chiefs. There was no chief for the whole tribe. In historical times seven major bands lived in Colorado: the Capote band lived in the San Luis Valley and the upper Rio Grande; the Mouache band ranged south along the Sangre de Cristos into New Mexico; the Weminuche band occupied the San Juan drainage; the Tabeguache (Uncompahgre) band, the Gunnison and Uncompahgre watersheds; the Grand River (Parianuc) band, the Colorado River area; the Yampa band lived near the river that shares their name; and the Uintah band, actually a Utah group, sometimes entered western Colorado. Yet other bands lived in Utah.

The Utes hunted deer, elk, mountain sheep, antelope, and unlike the Plains Indians, depended to a great degree on smaller animals, particularly jackrabbits. Bison ranged the Colorado parks and mountains, and the Utes often hunted them, too, with bows and arrows and thrusting spears. After acquiring the horse, the Utes often organized large buffalo-hunting parties to go out on the high plains, where they had to keep alert for enemy tribes. They gradually and increasingly adopted more of the ways of life of the plains.

Their plant foods were varied because they had an excellent, detailed knowledge of all that grew in their country. They prized the brown-skinned roots and tubers of the yampa plant, a member of the carrot family; they knew the many uses of the yucca; they dug the rich bulbs of the camas. Grass seeds,

Ute encampment near Denver, 1874. Photo by
W. H. Jackson. *Courtesy State Historical Society
of Colorado.*

many berries, and the little piñon pine nuts came in season,
and they had the tools and baskets to gather them.

They built small, round shelters of poles and brush like the
other tribes of the Great Basin, but at a very early date began
to use tepees with coverings of tanned elk or buffalo hide.
These could be moved in Plains Indian fashion on a dog or
horse travois. Summer shelters were frames covered with
shady branches arranged to let the breezes blow through.

Ute clothing was similar to that described for the Plains
Indians, but in addition to the Plains-style winter robes of
buffalo or elk hides, they wove blankets from long strips of
rabbit skin, a Great Basin custom. In summer women might
wear a short skirt made of shredded bark, in Great Basin style.

The Utes were skilled in fine decorated leather work, and
unlike the Plains Indians, they were adept at basketry, pro-
ducing well-made bowls, burden baskets, and women's caps,
all of which could have woven colored designs. They made
some undecorated earthenware, but most of their pottery was
traded from the Pueblos and Jicarilla Apaches.

Ute ceremonial life was marked by many dances, accompanied by music and songs. The Bear Dance, which took place
at the opening of the spring hunting season, when bears left
their winter dens, is the most noted of the ancient dances. The
Utes, like all Indians, love to listen to the significant, interest-

28

ing stories passed down in their oral tradition from one generation to the next. Their tales, like those of other Great Basin tribes, feature animal characters. According to one legend, the Bear Dance was first given to a Ute man in a dream. A bear taught him to dance, and the people continued to do the same dance each year. It was held in a large circular enclosure with a covered hole on the west side representing the bear's cave. Men and women dressed in their best clothes faced each other in two lines. The women chose partners from among the men, and then they danced in shuffling, swaying movements which recalled the way the bear would dance. The celebration lasted for about three days and three nights.

The Utes believed in a God, a great power both male and female which can be seen in the sun and which, like the sun's rays, extends through the universe. They also felt that there are many spirit personalities in the world associated with people, animals, and plants. A great figure in many Ute tales is Yohovits, the Coyote, who delights in playing tricks on others.

Ute medicine men, who had received special power through personal vigils, used their experience to help other members of the tribe retain their physical and mental health.

In early times the Utes were usually friendly neighbors of the other Shoshonean tribes, but enemies of the Plains Indians and Navajos. They visited the peaceful Pueblo Indians often as friendly traders, but sometimes as raiders. When the Comanches, northern relatives of the Utes, first arrived on the Colorado plains in the early eighteenth century, the Utes helped them drive out the Apaches, but around 1746 the Comanches and Utes became enemies and fought scattered battles for forty years. From that time on, the Utes developed a close association with the Jicarilla Apaches, and there were some intermarriages and adoptions between the two tribes. Some hostilities were directed against the northern Shoshones, mostly after the Whites began to make their presence felt in the mountain West.

Among the Utes' most important neighbors to the east and south were tribes speaking related languages of the Athapascan family—the Apaches and Navajos. The Athapascans came from the north beginning about A.D. 900 to 1200, leaving behind speakers of similar languages in Alaska and western Canada. By 1500, and probably much earlier, the Apaches controlled the Colorado plains, where they hunted buffalo on foot and planted crops along the river bottoms. Other Apache groups began to spread over New Mexico, Arizona, and west Texas, but those who stayed in Colorado for much of their history were among the ancestors of the Jicarilla Apaches, who still live just across the New Mexico line. Colorado's eastern half was Apache country up to the early eighteenth century, according to an interpretation of reliable Spanish records and archaeological discoveries. They were then forced to the south by the invading Comanches. In more recent times the Jicarilla Apaches have occupied the Sangre de Cristo mountains and the adjacent plains in southern Colorado and northeastern New Mexico.

The early Apaches lived in small bands, each headed by a chief chosen for his ability from among family leaders. From their former northern lands they had brought hunting skills learned in the forests and a superior weapon, the sinew-backed bow. On the plains, Apache men began to hunt the buffalo on foot, and Apache women learned how to plant and tend corn, beans, and squash, and how to gather and use wild plants of the plains. Their houses were sometimes earth lodges and often dome- or tepee-shaped pole-and-thatch dwellings, but the Eastern Apaches adopted the skin-covered tepee and the dog travois very early. In fact, the first known Spanish record of the Apaches classically describes the typical plains way of life before the horse. Apaches wore skin clothing and moccasins. They became skilled basket weavers and made some pottery. *Jicarilla* means "little basket" or "cup," although the name may refer to their homeland near the cup-shaped volcanic cone of Capulin mountain, near the northern border of New Mexico.

Apache ceremonies include songs with beautiful words, music, and dances with strikingly costumed and masked dancers. They are held to assure long life and health for people, and are led by medicine men who have the proper training and practice. One of the best known is the four-day coming-of-age ceremony for a young girl. The Jicarillas also had a ceremonial relay race which resembled a seasonal Pueblo event.

Jicarilla Apache and Navajo beliefs about the universe are very similar. They look on the whole natural world as full of life and inhabited by holy beings, offspring of the Sky and Earth, who personify animals and other aspects of nature. In

Apache hunters on the desert, 1879–1880s.
Courtesy Smithsonian Institution National
Anthropological Archives.

the distant past, it is said, people emerged onto the surface
of the earth by climbing a ladder through a hole from the underworld. Like all Indians, they feel close to nature and seek aid
from the power that they sense in the world.

During the seventeenth century the Apaches were in contact with the Spanish people of New Mexico, and from them,
or through other Indians, they acquired horses. The horse
offered new opportunities to the Apaches; they could hunt far
out onto the plains, and they could sometimes descend swiftly
in raids on Spanish or Indian villages. The name "Apache"
gradually came to arouse fear in the more settled peoples, but
this was not because the Apaches were more ferocious than
other people. As early Spanish explorers said of the Apaches,
"They are an intelligent people. . .They are a kind people and
not cruel. They make faithful friends."[1] The Spanish people
also found them "very crafty in war," but the Apaches' reputa-
tion as fighters and implacable enemies really comes from a
much later period when they were making their last desperate
fight for freedom against the overwhelming force of the United
States Army.

Originally identical in language and culture to the Apaches, the Navajos have had a somewhat different history, and the two tribes have developed differing ways of life. It is likely that while the Eastern Apache ancestors were moving south along the face of the Rockies, the forerunners of the Navajos and some of the Western Apaches were following a parallel route through Utah and western Colorado. Well before 1500 the Navajo heartland was located in northwestern New Mexico and adjoining sections of Colorado, Utah, and Arizona. The present Navajo Reservation directly adjoins Colorado on two sides without entering the state, but throughout historical times some Navajos have lived in southwestern Colorado. They have usually not been on good terms with the Utes, both tribes keeping an uneasy peace that was sometimes broken.

The Navajos, until very recently, had no general leadership for the whole tribe, but were organized in clans, each with its own territory in the mountains, canyons, and semideserts of the Colorado Plateau.

After their arrival in the Southwest, the Navajos took more enthusiastically to raising crops than any other Athapascan group, and became such a truly agricultural tribe that they were given a name, "Navajo," which means "people with cultivated fields" in the Tewa language. Their name for themselves is "Diné," meaning simply "the people." Navajo clothing in early times was made like that of the Apaches, but their dwellings were different. From the early earth lodge built on a framework of forked poles, they developed a polygonal hogan of logs and earth, with a cribbed roof. Summer shelters were arbors of leafy branches. Like the Apaches, they built small houses in which they took sweat baths in steam made by pouring water over hot rocks.

Navajo arts are deservedly well known. Although silversmithing is a recent development learned from the Mexicans around 1850, shell and turquoise jewelry was made in early times. Beautifully patterned weaving in colored wool, learned originally from the Spanish New Mexicans and the Pueblo Indians, dates back at least to the seventeenth century. Navajos used the coil technique in both basketry and pottery.

Navajo ceremonial art is truly impressive. The wonderful images of its ritual poetry combine with the unforgettable quality of its unique music. The visual art of the large sand painting that represents traditional events and holy people in many colors, the poetry, and the music are all designed to put the individual in harmony with the universe and restore physical and mental health. Only singers who have gone through a long and careful training, and have learned all the songs, stories, and paintings that are part of a single ceremony, are allowed to lead it.

Like the Utes and Apaches, the Navajos have an entertaining cycle of stories about animal characters and heroes in which Coyote, the trickster, often plays a major role.

Two Shoshonean groups, the Wind River Shoshones and their far-ranging relatives, the Comanches, occupied a section of northern Colorado before 1800. After that date the Comanches left, but the Shoshones remained. Shoshone country included all the land north of the Yampa River, North Park, and the mountains to the front range north of what is now Rocky Mountain National Park. The Shoshones were northern neighbors of the Utes, speaking a closely related language and sharing much of the same way of life. Besides northern Colorado, they occupied much of the basin and plateau country in Wyoming, up to the Yellowstone. The closely related Bannocks and Northern and Western Shoshones made their homes in Idaho and Nevada. They were hunters and gatherers, while the more easterly bands were specialized buffalo hunters— Great Basin Indians who had adopted much of the Plains culture.

An especially active, aggressive group of plains Shoshone bands which came to be called the Comanches began to move south into the Colorado plains after 1700. At first allied with the Utes, they attacked and drove out the Apaches. By 1727 the only Apaches left in the Central Plains were the Jicarillas, who had withdrawn to the south around the Sangre de Cristo mountains, and the Kiowa–Apaches, in the Black Hills of South Dakota. Between them, the Comanche bands continued to move south toward Texas, eastern New Mexico, Oklahoma, and southwestern Kansas. The Spanish New Mexicans first met the Comanches around 1705 and had them as troublesome eastern neighbors for many decades. In 1746 the uneasy Ute-Comanche alliance broke up, and the two related tribes fought each other sporadically during the last half of the eighteenth century. The Utes were now confined to the mountains and margins of the plains, where they developed their long-standing friendship with the Jicarilla Apaches. The northernmost Comanche band, called the Yamparikas, or "yampa root eaters," were reported in northern Colorado by Escalante in 1776. A force of Spanish soldiers and Ute allies under de Anza met them in several battles on the tributaries of the upper Arkansas River in central Colorado in 1779. The Comanches fought bravely, but many were killed, including the famous war chief Cuerno Verde, "Green Horn." After about 1800 Comanches ranged in the southeastern corner of Colorado, south of the lower Arkansas River.

After they moved from the Rocky Mountains into the seemingly endless sea of grass called the Great Plains, the Comanches completed their transition to the Plains Indian culture.

All the tribes that remain on our list of Colorado Indians—the Kiowa, Arapaho, and Cheyenne, as well as the visiting Pawnee and Sioux—were true Plains Indians.

The Kiowas speak a language all their own, although some linguists say that it might be distantly related to the Tanoan speech of certain pueblos in New Mexico. But the earliest historical location of the Kiowas cannot be placed anywhere near New Mexico. Their own traditions, which are very reliable (the Kiowas were one of the few tribes to keep pictorial calendars, though admittedly the surviving ones do not go back this far) place them in the Yellowstone country of Wyoming and western Montana in the seventeenth century. At that time they were a forest-dwelling tribe of the northern Rockies rather than a Plains Indian people. Near the beginning of the eighteenth century, however, they began to move out across the Yellowstone River and onto the plains of eastern Montana. Here they met the Crow tribe, who helped them transform into a Plains people. The Crows taught them how to ride horses, gave them the Sun Dance ceremony and the sacred doll Tai-Me that went with it, and encouraged them to settle in the Black Hills to the east of the Crows. This became the Kiowa's stronghold for many years, but they were also a mobile tribe, traveling long distances from the Black Hills to trade and visit with friendly tribes and to raid enemies.

In the Black Hills the Kiowas met an isolated band of Plains Apaches, who not only became Kiowa allies, but always traveled with them. This Apache group was in practice adopted into the larger tribe, even though they retained their Athapascan speech and usually had to communicate with the Kiowas through sign language. The group became known as the Kiowa-Apaches.

Around 1760, pressured by the invasion of Cheyennes and Sioux from the north and east, the Kiowas began to move south into eastern Wyoming and Colorado. Here they met the Comanches, with whom they fought for a generation and then made peace. From 1790 on, the Kiowas and Comanches were friendly tribes who occupied much the same territory. Together they moved south through Colorado into the southern Great Plains below the Arkansas River. The Kiowas continued to treat the southeastern section of Colorado as part of their greater tribal territory until they suffered disastrous defeats at the hands of the United States Army and other Indians during and just after the Civil War. The center of their lands in more recent times, and the place where their reservation was established, is in and near the Wichita Mountains of southwestern Oklahoma.

Both the Arapaho and Cheyenne languages are members of the Algonquian family. This large group of languages is spoken by a number of the tribes along the Atlantic coast from the Carolinas northward, through the Great Lakes region and much of Canada, and by the Blackfeet in Montana. The ancestors of the Arapaho and Cheyenne were members of woodland tribes who lived in villages and raised crops near the western end of Lake Superior and the headwaters of the Mississippi River in what is now Minnesota.

The Arapahoes were among the first to move toward the west, entering the Great Plains in the mid-seventeenth century or earlier. During the movement they became a pure hunting tribe and "lost the corn and the art of raising it." They did retain stories, traditions, and their belief in Manitou or Man-above, the Great Spirit, from their Great Lakes days. But in all other ways they became a Great Plains tribe, including their adopting the Sun Dance ceremony and the keeping of the sacred pipe.

Before 1800 the Arapahoes had gradually traveled west through North Dakota, Saskatchewan, and Montana, and some bands possibly visited Colorado. In the Black Hills they met the Cheyennes, who had also come west and settled in that area. The two tribes began a strong alliance which persisted from that time on. Between 1810 and 1820 the Arapahoes moved between the North Platte and Arkansas rivers, thus

Drying buffalo meat in an Arapaho camp, 1870.
*Courtesy Bureau of Indian Affairs in the National
Archives.*

occupying most of eastern Colorado, and they remained there
well into the period of White settlement. The Utes and Arapahoes became traditional enemies, the Utes holding the mountains and the Arapahoes the plains. Hunting and war parties
of each tribe often entered the recognized territory of the other,
and clashes resulted. By 1835 the Arapahoes had divided into
Northern and Southern groups. The northern group hunted
buffalo along the North Platte, while the southern group was
based near the Arkansas, where they often traded for horses
with the Mexicans and Americans. The South Platte area was
well known to both, and people from the two tribal sections
often visited each other or intermarried. Arapahoe County,
on the South Platte River, is appropriately named, although
it embraces only a small part of former Arapaho land. Many
places in Colorado are hallowed by Arapaho tradition, since
the Arapaho felt that waterfalls and other natural spectacles
were signs of the presence of the Great Spirit. In Canada, the
Arapaho and their close relatives, the Atsina or Gros Ventres,
a group that separated from the Arapahoes in the north, were
sometimes called Fall Indians or Waterfall Indians. Arapahoes call themselves Inuñaina, "Our People."

The allied Cheyennes are so called from a Sioux word,
Shahiyena, meaning "people whose language we cannot understand," but their own name was Tsitsistas, "people who are
alike." They left the Great Lakes area later than the Arapahoes,
and did not "lose the corn" so soon, as they settled in villages

Above Bear, a Southern Cheyenne, praying with
pipe. Photo by George Bird Grinnell. *Courtesy
Museum of the American Indian, Heye Foundation.*

along the Missouri River and continued their agricultural
ways for some time. But after 1760 they held the Black Hills,
with the Sioux as friendly neighbors. From this time on they
ranged across the plains. Eastern Colorado was part of their
territory, occupied also by the Arapahoes. Like them, the
Cheyennes were generally split into northern and southern
divisions after the 1830s. In both north and south the Cheyennes and Arapahoes were allies, but the southern association
of the two tribes was more close. At about the same time, the
sacred arrow bundle of the Cheyennes fell into the hands of the
Pawnees, and although some of the arrows were later recovered,
the incident has never been forgotten. The Cheyennes were
also enemies of the Kiowas, and the two tribes had many
battles until peace was finally made in 1840.

It may sound strange, but in such a warlike tribe the
government lay in the hands of a council of forty-four peace
chiefs. Each chief was an elder, as well as the head of a family.
He had to resign his membership in a warrior society before
entering his ten-year term on the council. The council elected
a head chief and four associate chiefs.

The greatest traditional story of the Cheyennes concerns a young hero, Sweet Medicine, who taught the people many of their ways and brought them blessings. Among these were the four sacred arrows, whose use was taught to Sweet Medicine by Maiyun, the Great Spirit. Two of the arrows had power over buffalo, and two had power against human enemies. They were preserved and renewed in sacred rituals to guard the prosperity of the tribe.

It is impossible to tell the history of the Colorado tribes without mentioning the Pawnees and the Sioux—two Plains tribes whose homes, properly speaking, were outside what was to become Colorado, but who entered it from time to time and had great influence on its history. Plains Indians were very mobile, particularly after acquiring horses, and trips of hundreds of miles from their homelands were quite common.

The Pawnees lived in central Nebraska and Kansas and spoke a Caddoan language related to the speech of the Wichitas and Arikaras. Unlike the Plains tribes so far discussed, the Pawnees were agriculturalists and remained so, although they also hunted seasonally. They lived in sturdy, circular earth lodges as large as fifty feet in diameter. They built near the rivers and planted their crops in the rich riverine soils. But farmers though they were, they were certainly not peaceful. Through early times, Pawnee raiding parties represented danger to Indians living in Colorado. There were no one-way trails; the Indians of the Colorado plains also journeyed east to challenge the Pawnees. Actually, the distances were not always great, since for generations some Pawnee villages were located just east of what became the Colorado line.

Since the North Platte River marked the southern edge of Sioux territory, and the Sioux were allied with the Cheyennes and Arapahoes, it is not surprising that groups of Sioux entered Colorado from time to time. The Sioux, so called in a French abbreviation of a name the Ojibwas gave their enemies, called themselves Dakota, Lakota, or Nakota, meaning "allies." This is an appropriate name, because the Sioux were really a large group of allied tribes speaking dialects of the Siouan language. Other Siouan speakers not allied to the Dakotas were the Crows, Assiniboins, Poncas, Osages and other Plains tribes, the Winnebagos of Wisconsin, and several tribes of Virginia, the Carolinas, and Georgia. The Sioux proper, with their seven divisions or "council fires," occupied most of South

Dakota and large parts of Nebraska, Wyoming, North Dakota, Montana, and Minnesota. The different Sioux groups met together annually to celebrate the Sun Dance and talk together in council. The "council fire" of Sioux that most directly affected Colorado history was the westernmost division, the Teton Sioux or Lakota. In particular, the Oglala band, which occupied the Black Hills and much of eastern Wyoming from the late eighteenth century, and the Brulé band, which ranged down to the North Platte River in Nebraska and beyond, affected Colorado's history. Like the Cheyennes and Arapahoes, the Sioux were formerly a woodland tribe of the western Great Lakes region. They moved onto the Plains during the eighteenth century, became buffalo hunters, and ceased their practice of agriculture. In the best known period of their history they were a warrior nation that carried out brave exploits against most of their neighbors while remaining at peace among themselves.

We have come to the end of our brief list of early Colorado Indian tribes, but it would be a mistake to think that we have listed all tribes represented in Colorado history. Individual members and family groups from many other tribes came to Colorado in earlier times as visitors, captives, or adopted members of local groups, and later as residents in rural and urban areas. The Navajo and Sioux are most numerous among Indians who live in Denver and other Colorado cities, but members of almost every tribe of the United States, including those in Alaska and many tribes of Canada and Mexico, have lived and do live in Colorado. If English, Irish, Italian, and Japanese descendants can all be called Coloradoans, then certainly any American Indian who lives in Colorado, irregardless of tribe, is a Colorado Indian in the best sense of those words.

The Strangers Came

When two different societies meet for the first time, the resulting conflicts are not a matter of battles alone. There is also a conflict of minds and hearts, and the attitudes and ideas of people toward each other affect their actions. The first White strangers to come to Colorado and the whole southwestern region were Spanish, and the first of that nationality to venture north were private conquerors seeking to enrich themselves. The colonists came later.

The first spontaneous act of American Indians toward strangers not known to be enemies was hospitality. In curiosity and friendship they took in the traveler and tried to learn about him. But news traveled far and fast among the American Indians. So when the first Spanish goldseekers approached Colorado, the story had already spread that strangers who rode on the backs of huge magic dogs, who had an insatiable hunger for the yellow metal, who had powerful weapons, and who, though trading honorably at times, also mistreated other people cruelly on occasion, had arrived in the south.

Thus, when Coronado came north in 1540 he was met by the Indians with caution, not open hospitality. The Pueblos were hostile, but found the Spanish weapons and tactics invincible. They were forced to give the conquerors food, shelter, information, and whatever else they asked, and those who resisted were killed (sometimes by burning), horribly dismembered, or enslaved. The only Colorado Indians who met Coronado were the Apaches of the eastern plains. Although it is not believed that the Spanish entered Colorado in 1540 (they may have just touched the southeastern corner), they did meet Indians who probably often ranged into the area. The Apaches, having heard the fate of the Pueblos, treated the Spanish men with cautious friendship and encouraged them to move out of Apache country as soon as possible. The historian of the expedition, Pedro de Castañeda, was fascinated by the Apaches' (or "Querechos") way of life. But the Coronado expedition was not seeking tribes of hunters and planters. Spanish conquerors

41

had already plundered Mexico City and the Inca cities of Peru, and now sought more golden cities to pillage.

Other Spanish adventurers came north during the next fifty years to trade, catch Indians for slaves, look for gold, or try to start unauthorized colonies, but none are known to have entered Colorado.

Great disruptions for the Indians began in 1598 when the first Spanish colonizers came to New Mexico, moved into one of the pueblos, and evicted the residents. These colonists were not like Coronado; they had come to stay. They were not gold-seekers (though they would have taken gold had they found any), but would-be landlords who wanted Indians to plow the soil and raise crops for them in this new country so much like parts of Spain. Soldiers who had been sent north to guard the Spanish frontier and priests whose greatest desire was to teach the Indians the observances of Christian worship and principles of Christian belief, were also among the colonizers.

The Pueblo Indians bravely resisted the imposition of a foreign culture. At first, certain pueblos fought the Spanish troops, but found their enemies strong and vindictive. For example, when Acoma Pueblo tried to resist the strangers, hundreds of Indians were killed, each surviving warrior had one foot cut off, and all survivors, men, women, and children, were forced into slavery. After their losses in battle the Pueblo Indians settled down to keep their way of life through passive resistance, secrecy, compromise where absolutely necessary, and to wait their chance to get rid of the conquerors. Spanish authorities were equally determined to change the Indian way of life in areas they considered essential; they were willing to do this with kindness and persuasion if possible, but used force if necessary.

The Indians of Colorado, the Apaches and Utes in particular, now found themselves on the outskirts of a Spanish colony, with new opportunities and dangers presented by the strangers. The northern Indians had long been accustomed to visiting the pueblos and trading their animal hides, dried meat, tallow, and salt for maize, other farm products, cotton blankets, pottery, and ornaments like turquoise. They continued to do so after Spanish rule was established and even found new trade items: steel knives and new agricultural products, metal objects, some of which could be refashioned into arrowheads, and flint-and-steel for making fire. The Spanish landlords would not sell their livestock, especially not horses. They had already learned the danger of mounted Indians in northern Mexico; they made it illegal for Pueblo Indians to ride horses and strictly prohibited any trade with Indians in guns and gunpowder. They were successful in keeping guns out of Indian hands for a long time, but with horses the case was different. The Apaches, with their Navajo relatives, and the Utes to some extent as well, found it necessary to raid Spanish farms and drive off sheep, cattle, and horses. Horses could also be obtained by trade from Indians of northern Mexico, some of whom were members of far-ranging Apache bands. Also, the wild horse, or *caballo cimarron*, had already appeared in scattered herds upon the plains and uplands to the south. By the mid-seventeenth century many Colorado Utes and Apaches had horses and were skilled riders.

The Spanish believed that they were bringing the Indians from a state of barbarism or savagery to civilization and Christianity. They thought that Indian culture had no value of its own, and that Indian religion was dark superstition or even ignorant worship of the devil. But once the Pueblo Indians had outwardly accepted the Roman Catholic forms of Christianity, had been made to build churches on the edges of their pueblos, and had become accustomed to providing forced labor for their Spanish overlords, they were regarded as entitled to some forms of protection under Spanish law.

A different Spanish attitude applied to the other tribes, who did not live in settled villages and were therefore thought to be nomadic savages. With such people the Spanish used the long experience of Europeans with northern barbarians, trying to keep them under control with gifts and demonstrations of strength until such time as they might be conquered, induced to settle into what the Spanish considered civilized life, and Christianized. In the meantime, the Spanish feeling was that any Indian was better off living in a Spanish colony, even as a slave, than with his or her own tribe, because he or she would learn useful work habits and could be taught Christian truths. Thus, economic and religious motives combined to condone the enslavement of Apaches, Navajos, and Utes, even though the King's law of faraway Spain had forbidden it. Spanish laws were not always obeyed by Spanish colonists, any more than American laws were later to be obeyed by undisciplined frontiersmen in the West. In 1638, Spanish governor Luis de

Rosas attacked a group of Utes, killing many and enslaving the rest. Apaches were also often attacked and enslaved, although such actions could be called into question under the Spanish system. Peace and friendship with bordering tribes was desirable to the Spanish at times, and agreements were made with the Utes in the 1670s and visits exchanged. The Apaches, then true horse-riding Indians, continued to alternate raids with peaceful trading visits.

Periodically, resistance to Spanish rule provoked the Pueblo Indians into action, and Taos Pueblo often served as a center of rebellion. This is significant because Taos was also one of the most important markets and points of contact with Plains Indians. In 1637, Taos and Jemez Indians killed the Spanish missionaries, burned their churches, and rather than submit to Spanish retaliation, fled to their Apache friends north of the Arkansas River in Colorado. There they built a new pueblo called El Cuartelejo, "the fort," by the Spanish. Its exact location is unknown, but it was on one of the northern Arkansas tributaries in eastern Colorado or western Kansas. Some Pueblo Indians stayed among the Apaches for a long time—at one point the Spanish complained they had been there for twenty-two years—and each tribe had a chance both to teach and to learn. Soon the Spanish were referring to all of southeastern Colorado as "El Cuartelejo," and its Athapascan inhabitants as "Cuartelejo Apaches." A northward expedition under Juan de Archuleta, the first White man known to have entered Colorado, visited El Cuartelejo and brought back a few Pueblo Indians, but not all, and Colorado continued to serve as a refuge for those who chose to flee from Spanish rule.

Indians won their freedom throughout New Mexico in the great Southwestern revolt, which simmered for several years and then broke out violently in October 1680 under the leadership of Popé, a medicine man from San Juan Pueblo. The revolt was centered among the Pueblo Indians, who bitterly resented Spanish attempts to change their way of life and, in particular, to wipe out their religion. Pueblo Indians had been willing to do their traditional dances to honor the new Catholic saints, but they could not easily take the beatings that were administered when they failed to attend Mass, or the burning of hundreds of their kachina masks and other sacred objects. During the revolt, all of the pueblos cooperated in a remarkable show of unity, and they received the help of the Apaches and Navajos as well. All the Spanish people were either killed, captured, or forced to flee south to El Paso, and all the possessions they left were either taken or destroyed. The Palace of the Governors in Santa Fe became a new Indian pueblo.

It is conceivable that the Spanish government might have written off New Mexico as too distant and hard to defend, but just at this time the French began to probe aggressively at the Spanish North American frontier from the east. The commission for the reconquest of New Mexico was presented to a new governor, Diego de Vargas, and within five years, aided by disunity among the Indians, he succeeded. During the reconquest, de Vargas entered Colorado by way of the Rio Chama and the San Luis Valley and contacted the Utes.

Many Pueblo Indians fled to the Navajos and Apaches to escape the reconquest. Some Navajos and Pueblos lived along the upper San Juan River in Colorado at that time, and El Cuartelejo became a center for refugees from Taos and Picuris under the leadership of their chief, Lorenzo.

It was to secure the return of these people and to check on rumors of French presence that Captain Juan de Ulibarri was sent north in 1706 with a small but well-equipped force. After travelling through friendly Jicarilla Apache country and being warned of the presence of hostile Comanches, Ulibarri reached the present site of Pueblo and then proceeded east to El Cuartelejo. There he found proof that the French trade in guns was reaching the Apaches through the Pawnees and was told that the French were not far to the northeast. In fact, the Apaches had met and defeated a French and Pawnee force not long before and had killed at least two of the French.

The combined threat of the French with their Pawnee allies and an active invasion of Utes and Comanches, along with appeals for protection by some of the Apaches, caused the Spanish to send more expeditions through Colorado. Governor Antonio de Valverde marched along the Arkansas River in 1717. Two years later, at Valverde's orders, Captain Pedro de Villasur crossed the Colorado plains, going from El Cuartelejo north to the South Platte, then down that river into present Nebraska, where the Pawnees killed Villasur and most of his troops.

We do not know exactly when the Indians of Colorado first met French traders, but the French had reached Kansas and were trading guns to the Comanches by 1725. In 1739 Pierre and Paul Mallet met only Comanches when they crossed eastern Colorado with a group of French traders, passing near La Junta and Raton in an unsuccessful attempt to set up trade with Santa Fe. In the middle third of the eighteenth century, French traders and trappers fanned out over the plains, providing the gun trade which was so eagerly sought by the Plains Indians, collecting furs, and serving as a source of disturbing rumors for the Spanish, who were trying to make peace with the Utes and Comanches. In 1750 the Utes, now at war against the Comanches, allied with the Spanish. Then, in 1763, resulting from a treaty signed in distant Europe, all the French claims to territory west of the Mississippi River passed into Spanish hands. The now friendly Utes allowed some Spanish exploring parties to pass through their country in Colorado. Juan Rivera crossed from the Dolores River to the Gunnison River on the western slope in 1765 and found some silver, but the discovery was not exploited. In 1776 Fathers Atanasio Dominguez and Silvestre Escalante traveled through Ute country looking unsuccessfully for a road to California and receiving hospitality and guidance from the Utes all through western Colorado.

An effective Spanish military intervention among the tribes of Colorado occurred in 1779, when Governor Juan Bautista de Anza, with Ute and Jicarilla Apache allies, pursued a band of Comanches headed by the renowned chief, Cuerno Verde. De Anza moved up through the San Luis Valley, across the upper Arkansas River and South Park, and then back south along the front range, capturing and burning the Comanche camp and killing the chief in a battle near present Rye, Colorado. The governor followed up his victory by negotiating a peace between the Utes and Comanches and settling the Comanches in a town, San Carlos, on the Arkansas River near present Pueblo. The town was soon deserted and the peace not well kept between the tribes. The Spanish also used the Utes as allies against the Navajos; a treaty was concluded to this effect in 1789, and a campaign was undertaken in 1804.

About this time the Colorado Indians began to meet a different kind of stranger, the "American." At first these people were hard to distinguish from the French because they were trappers and traders who sometimes traveled together and were likely to acquire Indian women as more or less permanent wives. But American trappers were not always friendly; they sometimes tended to "shoot first and ask questions later," and they drove hard bargains in trade. Eastern Colorado, as part of the great territory of Louisiana, had been retroceded by Spain to France in 1800, and three years later had been purchased by the young United States from France. This gave eastern Colorado to the United States, but a later agreement with Spain formalized the boundary at the Arkansas River. Lewis and Clark, accompanied by the Shoshone woman, Sacajawea, passed far to the north of Colorado, but Zebulon Pike in 1806 came up the Arkansas and into the San Luis Valley, where he was taken prisoner by the Spanish. Other official United States military expeditions came west under Long in 1820, Dodge in the 1830s, and Kearny and Fremont in the 1840s, but none were hostile to the Indians.

In response to the American presence, a Spanish fort was briefly established at Sangre de Cristo Pass in 1819, but Spanish rule was soon to end. In 1821, with the success of the revolution against Spain, twenty-five years of Mexican control began in the Southwest. Mexican law made citizens of Indians, Mestizos, and Whites alike. In the north the Mexicans continued to use some Indians, such as the Utes, as allies against more hostile groups. In spite of a prohibition against slavery in Mexican law, the capture and sale of children from the tribes on the northern frontier continued. Mexico granted large tracts of ranch land to private individuals in the 1830s and 1840s in northern New Mexico, and some of these included sections of Colorado, especially in the San Luis Valley and east of the Sangre de Cristo range. The Utes and Jicarilla Apaches were not excluded from their former lands, but often established their camps within the huge ranch "kingdoms." Some Indians were even used as ranch hands, since they were skilled horsemen.

Unlike the Spanish, the Mexican government encouraged trade with the Americans. In the 1820s American trappers infested Colorado, taking beaver from streams in every part of the state-to-be in such numbers that in 1824 Mexico City, alarmed, passed an ineffective law prohibiting beaver trapping.

When the Santa Fe Trail opened, one branch headed up the Arkansas River and then angled to the southwest over Raton Pass through territory where Whites might meet Indians of seven or eight different tribes. The other branch cut across the extreme corner of Colorado along the Cimarron River. One of the first trading posts in Colorado, Bent's Fort, was built in 1833 on the northern, or American, side of the Arkansas River a few miles downstream from where the Santa Fe Trail branched off to the south. Two of the owners, Charles and William Bent, became friends of the Indians, the Cheyennes in particular. They received the advice of Chief Yellow Wolf on the location of the fort. William married Owl Woman, daughter of Gray Thunder, the keeper of the medicine arrows. When Owl Woman died, her sister Yellow Woman became William's second wife. Charles became the first American governor of New Mexico, and William's sons, George and Charles, were later present at the Sand Creek massacre, where they chose to be Cheyennes. Other trading posts were soon built in Colorado: Forts Lupton, Jackson, Vasquez, and St. Vrain along the South Platte, all of which marked a trappers' trail running north and south parallel to the front range, and Forts Uncompahgre (Robidoux) and Crockett in western Colorado. These posts meant that Indians no longer had to leave Colorado to trade with non-Indians; they brought in buffalo robes and beaver pelts to exchange for items the traders could offer: axes and knives, rifles, lead and powder, textiles, beads, and whiskey, even though United States law prohibited the sale of alcohol to Indians.

International borders were of almost no concern to Indians at this time. Certainly the far-flung claims of distant nations had no effect on the Indians' feeling that their land was there to live upon and enjoy. But in the late 1840s, Colorado became part of the United States in treaties and in atlases, and it would not be long until the Indians began to suffer the practical effects of the American claim. In 1845, with the annexation of Texas, the United States acquired a hazy claim to central and southern Colorado, and won the rest in the Mexican War, which began a year later. The treaty of Guadalupe Hidalgo in 1848 gave the entire Southwest, including New Mexico and the last western section of Colorado, to the United States. The Comanches, Apaches, and Navajos, who had fought the Spanish New Mexicans, expected that the Americans, who had so recently been enemies of the Spanish-speaking people, would be friendly to them. However, this was not the case. The treaty ending the war guaranteed Mexican law in the Southwest and granted citizenship to Mexican citizens, not to frontier tribes.

48

The United States assumed the protection of the New Mexicans and the Pueblo Indians against other Indians. Meanwhile, the American frontier was not standing still, and even more important changes were to come.

Indian Removal

By the time Colorado became United States territory, federal Indian policy was already established and developing. In order to understand the relations between Indians and non-Indians in one state, it is necessary to understand the national picture. From colonial times major official decisions about Indians usually have been made at high levels in the government, not locally. When United States authority, military and civilian, was exerted upon Colorado Indians, Americans acted with experience gained from dealing with other tribes farther east. They also brought with them old prejudices, fears, and misconceptions.

The United States Constitution clearly implied that Indians were not citizens. When the population of the states was counted to determine representation in Congress, the Constitution excluded "Indians not taxed," even though three-fifths of the slaves were to be counted.[1] A special relationship between Indians and the government was recognized very early. The Constitution gave Congress the power of regulating commerce with Indian tribes and authority over all federal public lands. Thus, the responsibility for dealing with Indian tribes was given to the federal government, not to states or private citizens.

Congress had already asserted this responsibility even before the Constitution was written. A series of laws had forbidden any attempt by Americans to acquire Indian lands by settlement or purchase without congressional authority. The government wanted citizens to settle the western lands, but this was intended to be made possible by legal agreements with Indian tribes in "utmost good faith."[2] These agreements usually took the form of treaties. The first such treaty was signed by the United States and the Delawares during the Revolutionary War (1778). By that time the Delawares had been forced westward into Ohio from their original homes along the Delaware River. The Constitution gave the power to make treaties to the President with the "advice and consent"

51

of the Senate, and made treaties part of "the supreme law of the land."[3] Hundreds of treaties were eventually made with Indian tribes, but their provisions were often renegotiated, changed, or simply ignored by the United States government and citizens.

It was difficult for the government to force frontier citizens to observe laws and treaties. When miners or settlers moved onto Indian land, the intruders were seldom removed; instead, the government used its military and treaty-making powers to get the Indians to give up their land. Trouble between Whites and Indians in the frontier areas was so constant that many government people began to favor a radical policy to solve the Indian problem: removal of the Indians to lands out of the way of settlement. With the rapid movement of Americans westward, such a solution could only be temporary for the United States as a whole. However, removal seemed expedient and permanent for the non-Indians in a given area, because they could thus get rid of their Indian neighbors and take over the land and properties.

The Delawares are an example of Indian removal. The Treaty of 1778 had offered them statehood in what later became Ohio. Instead, they were pushed through Indiana and Illinois to a reservation in Kansas which also fell prey to people who wanted their land. They ended up in the part of Oklahoma that was supposed to remain Indian Territory forever.

The most famous case, however, is that of the Cherokees of the Georgia and Carolina mountains. The Cherokees had done more than any other tribe to adopt cultural elements from the Americans. One of their wise people, Sequoyah, had invented a script in which the Cherokee language could be written, and soon afterwards schools and a tribal newspaper were established. The tribe wrote a constitution and code of laws following the United States model and elected John Ross as principal chief; they also built White-style houses. Some Cherokees were prosperous farmers, and others became miners; in 1828 gold was discovered on their land in Georgia. Unfortunately, Andrew Jackson, the most powerful agitator for Indian removal, was elected President the same year. He encouraged Georgia citizens to work through their state government against the Cherokees. Georgia passed laws forbidding meetings of Cherokee courts and councils and prohibiting the Cherokees from mining gold on their own lands. In answer to two Cherokee appeals to the United States Supreme Court, Chief Justice John Marshall declared that the Cherokee Nation was not a "foreign state," but a "domestic dependent nation" whose "relation to the United States resembles that of a ward to his guardian."[4] Marshall declared the Georgia laws null and void, and affirmed the right of the Cherokees to their own land. Jackson is said to have replied, "John Marshall has made his decision, now let him enforce it." In the meantime, the President had pushed a bill through Congress authorizing the removal of the Cherokees and four other southeastern tribes to distant Oklahoma. Under conditions of great cruelty, in hunger and winter's cold, the Cherokees were driven west by American soldiers on the infamous "Trail of Tears." Of those who set out, about one-fourth, or 4,000 people, died along the way.

It is ironic that the first reports of gold in Colorado in the 1850s, which unleashed the tide of miners and settlers to the Pike's Peak goldfields and eventually doomed the Colorado Indians to suffer removal, were made by Delaware and Cherokee Indians who had gained mining experience in the East. The Cherokees were Lewis Ralston and John Beck, a preacher, who made their discovery while on their way to the California goldfields and later returned with others to Colorado. Fall Leaf, the Delaware, reported his discovery to people in Kansas, but did not return to Colorado himself.

The execution of United States Indian policy was in the hands of both military officers and civilian appointees from American independence onward. In 1824 the Bureau of Indian Affairs was created in the War Department, and a commissioner was appointed in 1832. In the year after the end of the Mexican War, 1849, the Bureau was moved to the new Department of the Interior, which also had responsibility for the territories and public lands. The B.I.A. and its commissioner remained under the Secretary of the Interior from that time on, steadily growing in power and influence over every aspect of the lives of Indians.

After 1848, United States Indian policy in Colorado was directed toward protecting the transcontinental routes to Oregon, California, and Santa Fe, safeguarding the settlers, and restricting the Indians to certain areas. Such restriction was accomplished through agreement and the distribution of gifts and rations when possible, and military action when thought to be necessary.

The policy of the Indians toward the United States varied from tribe to tribe. Generally, however, Indians wanted to preserve their existence and freedom, to accept offers of peace and friendship if they seemed sincere, but to resist the encroachments that soon began to threaten them. Some Indians believed that resistance should take the form of warfare. Others were sometimes willing to compromise in the presence of overwhelming American power, in the hope that they could save through conciliation and appeal to the conquerors' justice what seemed doomed to certain loss through war. Allied tribes, such as the Arapahoes and Cheyennes, could form a common policy, but enemy tribes never united against the common adversary.

The first treaty between the United States and a Colorado Indian tribe was concluded with the Utes in 1849, having been arranged by James S. Calhoun, a United States Indian agent, and signed by Quiziachigiate, principal chief, and twenty-seven other Utes. This treaty set no boundaries, but recognized United States law and sovereignty, promised that the Utes would stay in their "accustomed territory," permitted the United States to establish Indian agencies and military posts in Ute country, and promised the continuing friendship and peace to which the Utes had already agreed. During the Mexican War, William Gilpin had conferred with the Utes and led a campaign against their old enemies, the Navajos, in the San Juan basin of Colorado. Gilpin also fought the Comanches along the Arkansas River. A Ute agency was established at Taos in 1850 with John Greiner as agent, succeeded three years later by Kit Carson.

During that period settlements such as Costilla and San Luis were made on those northern fringes of New Mexico which later fell partly within Colorado. Fort Massachusetts was established near La Veta Pass in 1852 to protect these former Mexican citizens. In 1853 a military expedition under Captain John W. Gunnison crossed Colorado Ute country in search of a railroad route, but Gunnison was killed by Utes in Utah. The Utes were disturbed by American military presence and the northward movement of settlers, and in 1854 they and their Jicarilla Apache allies began a series of attacks on forts and settlements. The Ute leader in this war was Chief Tierra Blanca.

They took the trapper outpost, Fort Pueblo, killing fifteen men and capturing a woman and two children. American troops were sent north to relieve Fort Massachusetts and defeat the Utes; in an attack on a Ute camp near Salida forty warriors were killed. After several additional battles demonstrated that the United States commander, General John Garland, intended to crush all the Utes, the Capote and Mouache bands asked for peace and signed treaties that were not ratified by the Senate.

Mining camps such as Silver Plume affected change among Indian cultures in Colorado, particularly during the late 1850s and early 1860s. *Courtesy State Historical Society of Colorado.*

East of the mountains, treaties were signed with the United States by the Cheyennes and Arapahoes at Fort Laramie, Wyoming, in 1851 and by the Comanches and Kiowas at Fort Atkinson, Kansas, in 1853. These treaties were intended to guarantee peace and free movement for travelers along the Oregon and Santa Fe trails. In Colorado, the Arapahoes and Cheyennes were confirmed in their possession of the plains between the Arkansas River and the North Platte, while the Comanches and Kiowas were conceded to own the land south of the Arkansas. Annual provisions were to be given to the northern bands at Fort Laramie and to the southern bands at Bent's Fort. The Indian agent responsible for these agreements was Thomas ("Broken Hand") Fitzpatrick, and prominent among the Indian leaders was the Arapaho Chief, Cut Nose. The treaties were generally observed in Colorado during the early 1850s, but a few infractions occurred. Chiefs who counseled peace found it hard to control young warriors anxious to gain glory in raids, and wiser army commanders were not always present to check other officers who could develop an incident involving a stolen horse or cow into a full-scale battle. By 1857 hostile actions along the trails by both Indians and emigrants were fairly numerous, and the United States Army decided to make a show of force against the Indians, particularly the Cheyennes, on the Central Plains. In the summer of 1857, Colonel Edwin V. "Bull" Sumner led four companies up the North Platte to Fort Laramie and turned south into Colorado. Major John Sedgwick came up the Arkansas and along the front range with a similar force, meeting Sumner near the site of Greeley. The united command then moved eastward through the Cheyenne heartland into Kansas. No hostilities occurred in Colorado, but in a spectacular clash on the Salomon River in Kansas, the Cheyennes were defeated, and relative peace reigned as the news of gold discoveries traveled eastward the following year.

The Pike's Peak Gold Rush altered the whole picture for Colorado's Indians. Without warning, the plains were swarming with prospective miners heading west. Several new trails appeared, while buffalo and other wildlife were killed or driven away. New towns sprang up along the base of the front range and in the mountains—on land that belonged to the Indians by treaty. But it so happened that the first and largest American settlements were located on the strip of land where the plains meet the mountains—territory where both the Utes and Plains Indians traditionally hunted, and where they often clashed with each other. None of the tribes offered the strong objections to settlement in that marginal land which they might well have done had the settlements been in their heartlands. Instead, they accepted the fact that it was the newcomers, not their old rivals, who would be met there, and who might provide a buffer or screen. But complications soon appeared. Arapahoes sometimes left their wives and children in the relative safety of Denver while they ranged on war parties against the Utes.

Indians lived in Denver from the beginning. It has already been pointed out that some of the goldseekers were Indians from the east. Both Utes and Arapahoes came to Denver, and many old pictures of the city show an Indian encampment adjacent to the town, probably for trade and protection.

The early 1860s were a time of crisis in Indian-White relations. The extreme dislocations of the Civil War among the Americans added to the fears, anger, and willingness to seek quick, violent solutions. Like Indians, American settlers also came from many ethnic and cultural backgrounds. Some Whites were good, others were bad, and the government could not exercise control over the wide-ranging frontiersmen. In the best of times, the rapid American movement into Indian lands could not have gone on indefinitely without some new arrangement with the tribes. This was the object of the Treaty of Fort Wise (Fort Lyon), Colorado, hastily foisted on the Cheyennes led by Black Kettle and White Antelope, the Arapahoes led by Little Raven (Chief Hosa) and Left Hand, and other Indians in February 1861, at the very moment the Southern states were organizing their secession. This treaty, which never was accepted by Indians not present at the council. and which was repudiated by those who were, would have given the Arapahoes and Cheyennes a reservation of 600 square miles in eastern Colorado between Sand Creek and the Arkansas River, extending a bit south of the Arkansas west of the Purgatoire.

When Colorado became a Territory in 1861, John Evans, who became governor the following year, tried to get the Indians to obey the treaty. He held councils with chiefs and sent some of them on visits to the Great White Father to see the power and generosity of the United States government. But incidents between Whites and Indians in Colorado continued, often stirred up by soldiers or civilians who shared the feeling that the Indians should be driven away or that "the only good Indian is a dead Indian." However, one account which appeared in the Denver *Rocky Mountain News* in 1864 showed that some White people in Colorado were willing to be objective or even sympathetic to the Indians:

White men have undoubtedly been the aggressors. There are a lot of unprincipled scamps in the country who think that an Indian has no rights they are bound to respect. They steal Indian ponies and other property and if the owner objects they retaliate, likely as any way, by shooting him. This is the beginning of the trouble. Then it is represented as a dangerous outbreak on the part of the Indians and war follows. The Indian villages are broken up and their property destroyed; incited in the first place to hide the stealing of white men, and then encouraged and carried on to enable them to plunder *ad libitam.* The authorities are not to blame. They have no other course to pursue but to conquer a peace.[5]

The "authorities" were deeply concerned with "the necessity of extinguishing the Indians' title"[6] to land on which towns and mines stood, and believed that this would have to be done either by the peaceful removal of Indians to reservations, or by war and the extinction of the "Red Men." The settlers had come to Colorado with a firm prejudice already formed—that the Indians were doomed to vanish before the onward march of civilization, driven toward the west by the advancing frontier. Many stated the case in stronger terms, calling the Indians "unprincipled nomads" and "treacherous vagabonds" who should "be hunted to their doom like so many wolves."[7]

These attitudes could only be inflamed by reports, unfounded but widely circulated, that the Confederates were actively trying to arouse the Indians to attack the settlements, that Sioux Indians who had taken part in a violent uprising in Minnesota (they had killed scores of settlers after a delay in promised rations had reduced them to the point of starvation) were inciting the Colorado Indians to similar actions, or that the Arapahoes and Cheyennes were planning an imminent attack. Colorado military forces, reduced by the demands of the Civil War, were supplemented by citizen volunteers called up for shorter periods of service. What seems to have occurred

Members of a council held in Denver in September
1864. *Courtesy State Historical Society of Colorado.*

between 1861 and 1864 is that a series of military attacks on
Indian camps goaded the Plains Indians into retaliating by
raiding some farms and other outposts. In June 1864 Governor
Evans adopted a tactic often used in United States-Indian
conflicts, inviting all Indians who wished to be considered
"friendly" to come in and camp under the protection of military installations like Fort Lyon. All those who remained at
large would be considered "hostile." In August he called up
men for a hundred days' service in the Colorado Volunteers
and placed them under the command of Major John M. Chivington, who had been instrumental in turning back a Con-
federate invasion in New Mexico before it reached Colorado.
Chivington, an officer with political plans, was anxious to add
to his list of victories. Evans also issued a proclamation to
Colorado citizens, asking them to organize for their own defense
and saying:

> Patriotic citizens of Colorado: I again appeal to you to
> organize for defense of your homes and families against
> the merciless savages. . . . Any man who kills a hostile
> Indian is a patriot; but there are Indians who are friendly
> and to kill one of these will involve us in greater difficulty.
> It is important therefore to fight only the hostile, and no
> one has been or will be restrained from this.[8]

Black Kettle and other Cheyenne and Arapaho chiefs had decided to accept the governor's invitation to peace and came into Denver with Major Edward W. Wynkoop, commander at Fort Lyon, to meet with Evans and Chivington at Camp Weld. The Indians were told to surrender to Wynkoop at Fort Lyon with all their followers, and they did so in October. Major Scott J. Anthony, who replaced Wynkoop in early November, persuaded the Indians to move forty miles away to Sand Creek, where they remained peaceful and understood themselves to be under military protection.

Meanwhile, Chivington, in command of men whose period of service was about to run out, was being taunted in the press with charges of inactivity. He decided to make an unprovoked surprise attack on the Cheyennes and Arapahoes at Sand Creek. On the morning of November 29, 1864, one of the most infamous and controversial events in Colorado history took place. Some of the Indians saw the soldiers coming but could not believe that they were under attack until the shells began to explode and the soldiers, who were under orders to take no prisoners and to let no one escape alive, began to shoot them down. Black Kettle stood in front of his tepee under an American flag and the white flag of surrender, but those were ignored. He managed to escape, but his wife was severely wounded. White Antelope was shot down after he tried to surrender and died standing calmly, singing his death song:

"Nothing lives long
Except the earth and the mountains"[9]

Men, women, and children were killed indiscriminately and cruelly. No one knows how many died. Little Raven's village of Arapahoes was warned in time and managed to escape. Chivington said afterward, "All did nobly," but Sand Creek stands in history as a reminder that savagery in warfare is not limited to those who have been called "savages." Wild rejoicing among the non-Indian people of Colorado was replaced with uneasy questioning when the details of the massacre of a peaceful encampment became known. Chivington resigned before he could be court-martialed, but his political career was ended.

Sand Creek's result was to make the friendly Plains Indians hostile and to start a widespread war in which hundreds died, Indian and non-Indian. The Cheyennes and Arapahoes allied themselves with the Sioux and attacked military posts and settlements along the South Platte and across the plains. They captured the town of Julesburg, plundered the supply depot there, and attacked nearby Fort Sedgwick. Communications were disrupted, wagon trains were attacked, and Colorado was plunged into a state of emergency, martial law, and economic crisis.

Raids continued to penetrate the outskirts of some Colorado towns until 1869. Meanwhile, government officials tried to apologize for the Sand Creek massacre, make peace, and sign treaties, but some Colorado residents made loud calls for the total extermination of Indians.

Two treaties were signed at Medicine Lodge, Kansas, in 1867 in an attempt to establish peace on the southern plains with the Kiowas, Comanches, Apaches, Arapahoes, and Cheyennes. The Indians were to settle on reservations in Kansas and Oklahoma, while still retaining the right to hunt in the uninhabited portions of the land they were to surrender. But the treaties were not effective because the Indians refused to be confined as yet to the reservations, and they were continually irritated by the pressures of the frontier. The fighting became very intense in 1868. One of the incidents of that year was the famous Beecher Island fight in northeastern Colorado, in which Major George A. Forsyth and fifty experienced frontiersmen were surrounded for nine days and repeatedly attacked by Northern Cheyenne and Sioux warriors led by Chief Roman Nose, who was killed in the battle. Black Kettle also died in 1868, the victim of another surprise attack on his village on the Washita River in Oklahoma. Some of the Southern Cheyenne Dog Soldiers, a warrior society, managed to return to the South Platte valley with Chief Tall Bull, but were overtaken by Major Eugene A. Carr's troops and Pawnee allies on July 11, 1869, and defeated in the fierce Battle of Summit Springs, the last battle against the Plains Indians in Colorado. What many Colorado citizens had desired—the removal of the Cheyennes and Arapahoes (and of the Comanches, Kiowas, and Kiowa-Apaches as well)—had been accomplished by United States military force. Due to the failure of the Treaty of Fort Wise, eastern Colorado had become virtually "free of Indians."

It was also to become free of buffalo. The Union Pacific Railroad, completed through southern Wyoming in 1869, effectively divided the buffalo on the plains into northern and southern herds. The southern herd, including buffalo on the Colorado plains, was systematically slaughtered by commercial hide hunters between 1871 and 1874, a process coinciding with and helping to provoke the last war with the southern Plains Indians in 1874 and 1875 (which did not involve Colorado). The northern herd, except for a few remnants in the Yellowstone, was also hunted to extinction within another decade. The last unprotected wild buffalo known to have existed in the United States were a cow, a calf, and two bulls killed in 1897 in Lost Park, Colorado. Many military and civilian officials saw the extermination of the buffalo as a form of warfare against the Indians, and as the only means of finally confining them to the reservations and forcing them to give up their old, free way of life.

During this time the Utes remained at peace, and when their enemies, the Arapahoes, were gone from Denver, they began to come more often to camp nearby and trade. For a time the Ute bands remained independent and secure in their beautiful mountains. Although most of them wanted to have little to do with the Whites, a leader who arose among the Uncompahgre (Tabeguache) Utes—Chief Ouray—believed that some kind of understanding would have to be reached with the United States government. He wanted to make a treaty that would save the best part of his people's land. Ouray, whose Ute name means "Arrow," had lived in New Mexico and witnessed the United States' conquest. His mother was a Jicarilla Apache, and he knew the Spanish-speaking people as well as the Americans. In 1863, with the help of Indian Agent Lafayette Head, he arranged a treaty between his own band and Governor Evans that guaranteed the Uncompahgres' traditional lands, but this was superseded by an even more advantageous agreement, the Great Ute Treaty of 1868. For the negotiations he made a second trip to Washington, D.C. (his first trip occurred after the 1863 treaty). Accompanying him were chiefs of the Northern and Southern Utes, including Jack, Sowerwick, and Piah of the White River band and Kaneache of the Mouaches, as well as Kit Carson and Governor Alexander Cameron Hunt representing the United States. They were introduced to President Andrew Johnson and General Ulysses S. Grant, soon to be elected president. The treaty was relatively fair; although it deprived the Utes of the San Luis Valley and the central Colorado Rockies, it left them with a reservation

Ankatosh, Wa-rets (standing, left), Ouray (seated in center), Shavano (standing, right), and Guero. Ouray, or The Arrow, was an important headman of the Uncompahgre Ute band, as was his father. His mother was a Jicarilla Apache. Ouray was born in 1833 and died in 1880. Photo taken in Washington, D. C., in 1868. *Courtesy Smithsonian Institution National Anthropological Archives.*

covering about one quarter of Colorado Territory, an area bigger than several eastern states, stretching from just west of the present town of Gunnison to the Utah line and from the White River drainage on the north to New Mexico on the south.

Two agencies were established for the Utes pursuant to this treaty, the northern one at White River and the southern one to be moved from Conejos, where Lafayette Head had served as agent, to the Los Pinos River. When the Uncompahgre band refused to go farther south than the area around Cochetopa Pass, the agency was founded there, and a tributary of Cochetopa Creek was renamed the "Los Pinos" to satisfy legalities, even though it was not within the reservation. This agency was later (1874) moved to the Uncompahgre River, home of Ouray's band, but the name, "Los Pinos Agency," was retained.

The Senate ratified the treaty, but it was to be the last for the Utes. The year 1868 was a "vintage year" for treaties; important ones were also signed by the Sioux and Navajo. But Congress was impatient with the process of treaty making. The treaties were negotiated by the executive branch and submitted to the Senate for advice and consent; the House of Representatives was not required to pass them. But the treaties often contained solemn promises to deliver annuities of food, clothing, tools, or cash to erect buildings, and to provide services such as education, all of which depended for appropriations on the House of Representatives, the arm of Congress holding the purse strings. House failure to keep promises made by the President and Senate caused much trouble with the Indians. In 1871 a law was enacted ending the making of treaties with Indian tribes, although recognizing the legality of the treaties already made. From that time on, federal actions regarding Indians would be formalized through acts of Congress, passed by both houses, and signed by the President.

Not long after the treaty of 1868, a gold rush to the San Juan mountains inside the Great Ute reservation was under way. Under the terms of the treaty, the United States government should have forced the miners to leave, but this was politically impossible. United States troops would not be used against United States citizens to defend Indian rights. Instead, Felix Brunot was appointed to negotiate a new agreement with the Utes.

Brunot, an idealistic Episcopalian churchman, was an excellent representative of President Grant's "Peace Policy" toward American Indians. Grant had decided to use negotiation, rather than warfare, whenever possible. The Indians would be kept on reservations administered by religious people interested in Indian welfare and desirous of teaching them. Grant even appointed as Indian Commissioner the only Indian to hold the office in the nineteenth century—Eli S. Parker, a Seneca who had been Grant's staff officer. A Board of Indian Commissioners, a nonpartisan body of distinguished reformers, was created to advise the President on Indian issues. Felix Brunot was chairman of that new board.

Southern Utes during Boulder's semicentennial in November 1909. Left to right, standing, are: Capt. Charles Christy, Pee Viggi, Scout, Tony Buck, Maurice, Buckskin Charley, Edwin Cloud, Acapore, and Red Dog. *Courtesy State Historical Society of Colorado.*

Ouray did not want to surrender more Ute land, but he was still convinced that cooperation with the United States government was the best way for his people, rather than the stubborn warlike opposition which had resulted only in loss of life and removal for other tribes. So he signed the Brunot Agreement in 1873, which turned over about 6000 square miles of Ute land to the miners, almost one quarter of the entire reservation of 1868. The Utes were left with the northern section, along with a twenty-mile-wide strip down the western border of Colorado and a fifteen-mile-wide strip along the southern border. In addition, the agreement recognized Ouray as head chief of the entire Ute nation, and granted him an annual salary of one thousand dollars for ten years.

In the second half of the nineteenth century, white people who considered themselves friends of Indians were in favor of assimilation, that is, making the Indians become as much like United States citizens as possible. Since America was predominantly rural, they wanted to encourage Indians to become independent small farmers. Reformers had been urging that Indians should be allowed to select individual allotments of farmland that could be held in private ownership, as citizens were allowed to do by the Homestead Act of 1862. A provision permitting this practice had been inserted into the 1868 Ute treaty. Ouray decided to show his people that it was possible for them to adjust to White ways successfully. Even though both he and they would have preferred to live in the traditional ways—riding horses, hunting, and living on the plentiful gifts of the untilled earth—he felt strongly that they must change to save themselves. So, as an example to all Utes, he took a farm of 160 acres not far south of present Montrose and moved into a small house provided by the government. He and his wife, the dignified and resourceful Chipeta, adopted White dress and furnishings, all the way to china, silver teapots, and curtains. Outside, sheep grazed and crops flourished. For a time, the way of peace was prosperous.

The summer of 1876, the centennial year of United States Independence, brought two important pieces of news that would profoundly affect the Utes, whether they realized it or not. In early July Colorado's citizens approved the constitution for their new state and heard that on June 25 General George Armstrong Custer and 264 men of his command had been wiped out in battle by the Sioux and Northern Cheyenne in Montana. Certain citizens in the new state, some of them powerful, did not like the fact that out of one hundred thousand square miles, twenty thousand were occupied by a proud and independent Indian tribe. While these people might at times give lip service to the popular idea of Indian assimilation, they resented successful examples of it—like Ouray—and really preferred the older practice of Indian removal to make Colorado truly Indian-free. They agitated loudly for the removal of the Utes to Indian Territory, or to Utah. Colorado's voice in national politics became strong in 1876 and 1880, when the state's votes provided the winning margin for successful presidential candidates. Congress approved a commission to negotiate for Ute removal from Colorado in 1878, but when an agreement was submitted to locate the Southern Utes on a smaller reservation in Colorado's San Juan mountains, outside the mining district, the Utes' enemies were so intent on consolidating all the Utes for removal that Congress rejected the agreement.

Some Utes were moved *into* Colorado in 1878. The part of the Mouache band that had been living on the Maxwell ranch near Taos, New Mexico, was removed to the southern strip of the Colorado reservation. An agency was established for them, the Capotes and the Weminuches, at Ignacio on the Los Pinos River. An agency now finally stood on the banks of that river, as the treaty had stated ten years before. At the same time, Fort Lewis was located at Pagosa Springs (Pagosa means "hot springs" in Ute) to establish a military presence near the southern Utes. The Jicarilla Apaches, who had been living alongside the Taos Mouaches, had already been moved to the Tierra Amarilla region just over the New Mexico line from the Ute reservation. Their reservation was established, covering some of its present area, the following year.

Also, the Northern Cheyennes fled from their Oklahoma reservation in 1878. In spite of the determined attempts of the United States Army to stop them, the Cheyennes managed to return to northern lands they had known and loved. This flight, celebrated in the book and film *Cheyenne Autumn*, [10] passed through Kansas and Nebraska, just east of the Colorado line. Memories of the Custer battle were still fresh, and many Colorado citizens were uneasy.

During that same year, Nathan Meeker was appointed agent of the Northern Utes at White River through the good offices of Senator Henry Moore Teller of Colorado. Meeker, the founder of Greeley, was a utopian idealist who wanted to bring the Utes from their old ways to agrarian civilization as quickly as possible. He probably did not need the senator's urging to think that he could "in a short time make great improvements in the condition of the Indians." Teller had written him in these words, adding, "I have an idea you are the man to do it." [11] The Utes were friendly and cooperative at first, but determined to stay where they were and keep the way of life they had always known. Chiefs like Jack and Douglas were strongly traditional, and even though they respected Ouray—and the important White River medicine man, Johnson, was the husband of Ouray's sister, Susan—they did not share his eagerness to adopt White customs. Ute children would not stay in school, and the young men persisted in preferring horse racing to cultivation. As Meeker's frustration grew at what he saw as Ute obstinacy, he began using threats. If the Utes did not cooperate, he intimated, the Whites would take their land. He had some of the best horse pastures plowed up.

The Ute defiance of all his efforts frightened Meeker, and he called for federal troops to assist him. Johnson, enraged by something the agent had said, handled Meeker roughly without hurting him seriously. Consequently, the army sent in a detachment headed by Major Thomas Tipton Thornburgh, a commander who had recently taken part in the unsuccessful attempt to stop the Northern Cheyenne escape. Chief Jack and the other White River Utes, now seriously threatened, prepared to intercept the troops as soon as they entered the reservation. At the last moment the Utes agreed to a conference at the agency with Thornburgh, accompanied only by five soldiers. Thornburgh, however, changed his mind and advanced with a column of cavalry. The Utes surprised them at Milk Creek, killing Thornburgh and several others and putting the remaining soldiers under siege. On the fourth day, a group of Negro cavalrymen arrived under Captain Francis S. Dodge, who had been in Middle Park investigating unfounded reports that the Utes had been starting forest fires in the Rockies during that unusually dry summer. Dodge did not have enough men to raise the siege, however. It was not until the seventh day, when Colonel Wesley Merritt arrived with four companies of cavalry and some foot soldiers, that the siege was lifted.

Meanwhile, the White River Utes had attacked the agency, killing Nathan Meeker and all other male employees and taking Mrs. Meeker, her daughter, and another woman into captivity. Susan, who had once been rescued by cavalry soldiers from a band of Arapahoes, spoke on behalf of the White women and possibly saved them from death or treatment worse than they actually received.[12]

Rather than pressing the military campaign against the Utes, Secretary of the Interior Carl Schurz decided to work peacefully through Chief Ouray and General Charles Adams, a former Indian agent of German descent who had developed sympathy and understanding for the Utes. Adams traveled to Grand Mesa, where the women were being held captive, accompanied by several Utes including Sapovanero and Shavano (Ouray was too ill to travel), and they won the release of the prisoners and the agreement of the White River Utes to stop fighting.

Although some citizens demanded that the Utes who murdered the men at the agency and violated the women captives should be brought to justice, Ouray insisted that they could not be given a fair trial in Colorado. Finally, none were tried, although Douglas was briefly imprisoned. The people of Colorado were much more interested in having the Utes removed from the state, and the Meeker-Thornburgh incidents had provided the excuse they had been seeking. Negotiations were begun immediately for a new Ute agreement which would open most of the vast Ute reservation to sale and settlement by United States citizens.

The agreement was approved in 1880 by Congress and signed by more than three-fourths of the adult male Utes. According to its terms, the White River Utes would move to a reservation in Utah, the Uncompahgres to individual allotments near the Grand (Colorado) River, and the Southern Utes to allotments along the La Plata River from near Hesperus, Colorado, south into New Mexico. Before these terms could be carried out, Ouray died, knowing that his life's work had failed. Disgusted by what he saw as lack of good faith by those he had considered his friends, he abandoned White-style clothes and resumed traditional Ute wear before his death. Chipeta gave away the house and farm, along with almost every vestige of White ways, remarried, and lived in a traditional tepee in her beloved mountains for at least part of every year until her own death in 1924.

The White River Utes moved to Utah in 1881. In the same year, Ouray's own band, the Uncompahgres, refused to take allotments on the Grand River, and were escorted to the same Utah reservation by Colonel Ranald S. Mackenzie's soldiers from Fort Garland.

This left only the Southern Utes in Colorado. Fort Lewis was moved to Hesperus, near the La Plata area designated in the 1880 agreement. But the area seemed unsuitable for farm allotments. Also, the Denver and Rio Grande Railroad had reached Durango, and pressure was growing to have the Southern Utes entirely removed from the state to a new reservation in San Juan County, an isolated corner of Utah. Bills to accomplish this removal were introduced in Congress almost every year between 1886 and 1894, but all failed.

The political climate was changing toward Indians, including the Utes. "Friends of Indians," who favored Indian assimilation into the dominant society in America through education and allotment of land, were growing stronger, and the old advocates of Indian removal were losing momentum.

Helen Hunt Jackson, a resident of Colorado Springs, had done some careful research on the history of United States-Indian relations, and wrote an influential book, *Century of Dishonor*, published in 1881. As well as demonstrating that the United States government had often treated Indian tribes with bad faith, breaking many treaties, the book described massacres and other acts of violence by non-Indian Americans against Indians. Three years later Helen Hunt Jackson completed a novel, *Ramona*, a sympathetic portrayal of the California Indians she had been invited to study. In Colorado, she attacked the conduct of the soldiers at the Sand Creek Massacre, and spoke out strongly in defense of the Utes. She aroused outspoken friends and antagonists, the latter including William N. Byers, a former newspaper editor.

In the early 1880s several important organizations were founded to further Indian causes. Most of these, like the Indian Rights Association, favored Indian assimilation through education and the ownership of small farms. Like the Indians' enemies, these friends believed that the Indians were bound to disappear. But they thought that this disappearance should occur gradually, while Indians' rights were protected. Many of them favored making the Indians citizens.

The friends of Indians managed to get Congress to pass the General Allotment Act in 1887, sponsored by Senator Henry L. Dawes and often called the Dawes Act, a law providing that Indian reservation land, formerly held in trust for the whole tribe, should be divided. Each member of the tribe would receive land (heads of families usually getting 160 acres), called an "allotment." After twenty-five years, the individual Indian could receive both the private title to his land and citizenship. Since the law also provided that the land left over after all members of the tribe had received allotments was "surplus" land, to be purchased by the United States government and opened to non-Indian settlement, it was warmly supported by greedy people who saw the chance to enrich themselves on Indian land.

Alone among the organizations of Indians' friends, the National Indian Defense Association and the journal, *Council Fire*, opposed allotment and the destruction of tribal life that it would bring. *Council Fire* had been founded by Alfred B. Meacham, a man who, although seriously wounded by Modoc Indians in California, had nonetheless devoted himself to the cause of Indian rights. His work was continued by Theodore A. Bland. As a member of the commission charged with obtaining Ute signatures on the 1880 agreement, Meacham had delayed Ute removal and tried to keep land speculators away from the Indians.

Colorado's political leaders pushed hard for removal of the Southern Utes from the state, but they failed, in spite of the fact that Senator Teller, who favored that policy, was Secretary of the Interior from 1882 to 1885. The Indian Rights Association and representatives of other western states lobbied to keep the remaining Utes in Colorado, and as it became evident that Utah Territory, too, was about to become a state, the voices of ranchers in the proposed Utah reservation were increasingly heard.

The reformers had won. In 1895 the Hunter Act passed in Congress and was signed by President Grover Cleveland. This law set aside the southern strip of the old reservation in southwestern Colorado as the Southern Ute reservation and provided that individual allotments of land should be made in a way virtually identical with the Dawes Act. The Southern Utes were reluctant. Though willing to accept the reservation, the tribe split over the question of allotment. Chief Ignacio and his Weminuche band completely refused to take allotments, and although the government did not usually allow Indians to have a choice in such matters, in this case they let Ignacio have his way. The Weminuches and a few others moved to the western part of the new reservation, near Ute Mountain, and the government founded a subagency for them at Navajo Springs, south of Cortez, in 1897. Later, the reservation was split in two; the western, nonallotted half becoming the Ute Mountain Ute reservation and the eastern half, where the Mouache and Capote bands lived, remaining the Southern Ute reservation. By 1899 allotment of the eastern reservation had been completed, assigning less than 75,000 acres of land to individual Indians. President William McKinley then threw open the rest of the reservation, more than 500,000 acres, to non-Indian settlement. Reservation life, with its insistent demands that old ways be sacrificed to the new, had begun for the Utes in Colorado.

Maps depicting Indian settlement patterns in Colorado.

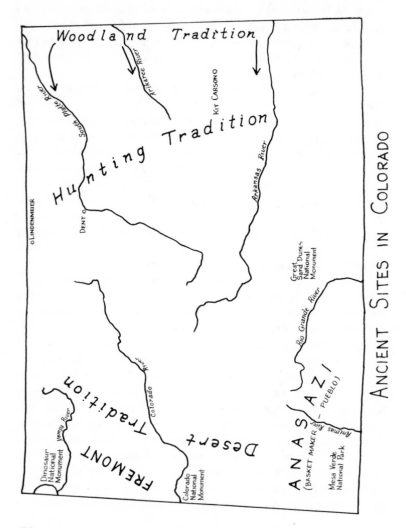

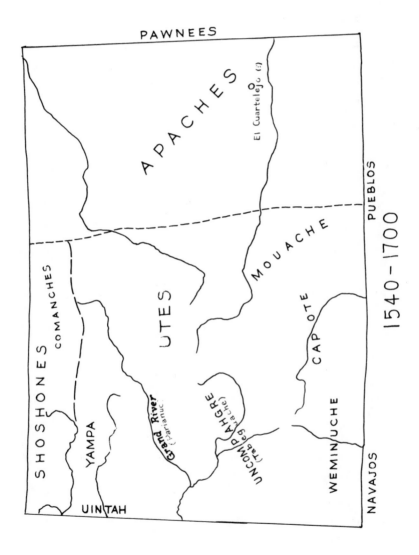

PAWNEES

APACHES

El Cuartelejo (?)

PUEBLOS

1540 - 1700

SHOSHONES

COMANCHES

UTES

MOUACHE

CAP OTE

YAMPA

Grand River
(Parianuc)

UNCOMPAHGRE
(Tabeguache)

WEMINUCHE

NAVAJOS

UINTAH

73

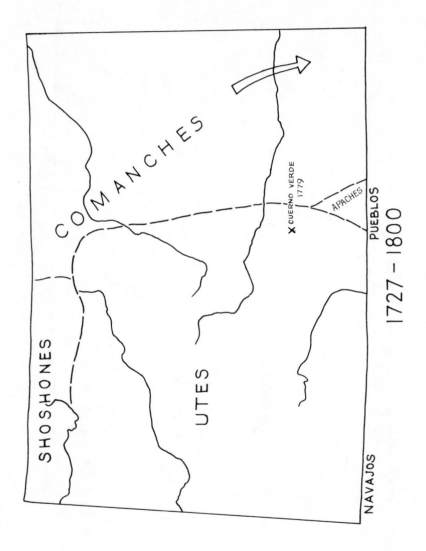

SHOSHONES

COMANCHES

UTES

CUERNO VERDE
1779

APACHES

PUEBLOS

NAVAJOS

1727 – 1800

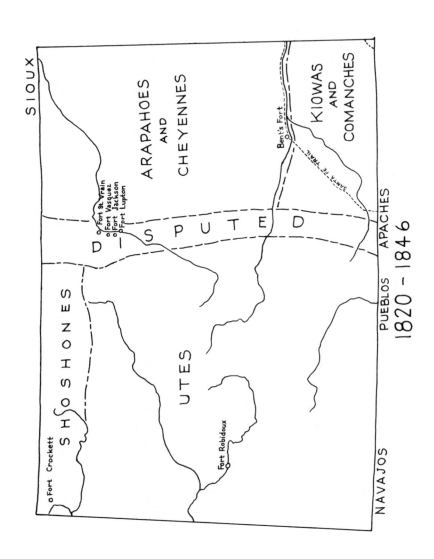

SIOUX

ARAPAHOES
AND
CHEYENNES

oFort St. Vrain
oFort Vasquez
oFort Jackson
oFort Lupton

Bent's Fort

KIOWAS
AND
COMANCHES

SANTA FE TRAIL

D I S P U T E D

SHOSHONES

oFort Crockett

UTES

Fort Robidoux

NAVAJOS

PUEBLOS

APACHES

1820 - 1846

1848-1879

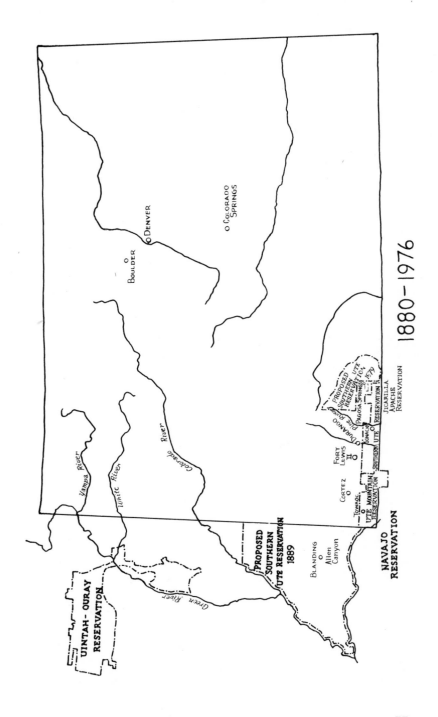

1880–1976

BOULDER O

DENVER O

COLORADO SPRINGS O

Yampa River

White River

Colorado River

Green River

UINTAH- OURAY RESERVATION.

PROPOSED SOUTHERN UTE RESERVATION 1889

BLANDING O

Allen Canyon

PROPOSED SOUTHERN UTE RESERVATION

PAGOSA SPRINGS

JICARILLA APACHE RESERVATION

DURANGO O

Pine River

IGNACIO O

SOUTHERN UTE RESERVATION

FORT LEWIS O

CORTEZ O

TOWAOC O

UTE MOUNTAIN RESERVATION

NAVAJO RESERVATION

Reservation Life

The Utes kept their tribal loyalties and worked with their own tribal leadership after their reservations had been established. After the death of Ouray, the chief of the Southern Utes was Buckskin Charley (Charles Buck, or Sapiah), Ouray's own choice. Serving until his death in 1936, Buckskin Charley gave his tribe the benefit of his experienced leadership for well over fifty years, respected by the Whites and trusted by his own people. He protected the interests of the Utes, believed strongly in their traditions, and always kept peace between them and their neighbors. Another important Southern Ute leader was the Capote chief, Severo, who lived until 1913.

Ignacio, who led the Weminuche Utes west to Ute Mountain, remained their chief all his life. He died in 1913. Other chiefs at Ute Mountain were Mariano and Redrock. Both the Southern Utes and Ute Mountain Utes had tribal councils composed of a small number of elders who discussed matters of importance and tried to agree on a course of action whenever necessary.

Among American Indians, the Utes have been noted for their determination to defend their own interests, all the way to Washington if need be, and for their knowledgeable use of United States courts. As early as 1896, Colorado's Southern Utes and Utah's Northern Utes organized the Confederated Bands of Ute Indians to take legal action in obtaining fair financial compensation for the lands taken from them. Through their contacts with Americans, and earlier with their Spanish New Mexican neighbors, the Utes had come to understand the importance of money and the uses of litigation. They hired lawyers and began a long, but ultimately successful, legal fight. The first judgment in their favor came in 1910 from the United States Court of Claims, which found that the government owed the Utes about $3,300,000 in payment for land taken as government reserves. Although the Utes were a small group and were at a disadvantage in dealing with a powerful government that often failed to heed them, this is only one example

Consolidated Ute Agency, 1925. *Courtesy State Historical Society of Colorado.*

of several incidents in which they finally won some measure of justice.

The Bureau of Indian Affairs was represented on each reservation by an agent (later called a superintendent) and his staff. After 1896, the Colorado Utes had two agents, one at Ignacio on the Southern Ute reservation and the other at Navajo Springs on the Ute Mountain reservation. From 1904 to 1910, the latter reservation was administered by the superintendent of Fort Lewis Indian School. In 1906 Mesa Verde National Park was created by Congress to protect the most important archeological sites of the Anasazi Pueblo Indians in Colorado. A section of the park consisted of land taken from the Ute Mountain reservation, but a much larger area was added to the reservation as compensation. In 1914 government facilities at Ute Mountain were moved from Navajo Springs to the present location at Towaoc. After the First World War the Consolidated Ute Agency, with administrative concern for both reservations, was centered at Ignacio.

The executive branch of the United States government made sweeping changes in the Southern Ute land base; a presidential order in 1915 added a few hundred acres to the reservation, and another in 1916 subtracted 64,560 acres for a naval oil shale reserve, although the latter order was subsequently rescinded.

The agents, or superintendents, generally regarded themselves as "in charge" of the reservations. They had considerable power, and at times ignored the wishes of the chiefs and tribal councils. The Utes found ways of resisting the agents, sometimes carrying complaints to Washington when they could not win reasonable compromises on the local level, or when they discovered that the agent was trying to cheat them.

Government administrators seldom stayed long at the Indian agencies in Colorado. During the first fifty years of the Southern Ute reservation, for example, there were twenty-two different agents or superintendents. Under these circumstances, even well-meaning agents could not get to know the Utes well, and some agents were incompetent or dishonest. The Utes' intelligence and ingenuity were taxed by a series of United States administrators who took a paternalistic attitude toward them and ordered them to follow the program established by the government. Throughout the first half of the twentieth century, an important part of this program was intended to make all the Ute men into farmers, or at least herdsmen. Whether this was a wise policy, since it involved a complete alteration of Ute customs against their own wishes, or whether it could ever have been a complete success considering the available land and the state of the local economy, was not an issue for the agents. They were only attempting to carry out policies established in Washington as general policy for almost all Indian reservations. Other elements of the government program were intended to teach Ute children the English language and vocational skills (farming for the boys and homemaking for the girls) and to provide medical attention, housing, and law enforcement (through Indian police) as economically as possible. The agent also controlled Indian finances, not only the annual federal appropriations, but also the tribal funds and the money belonging to individual Indians in bank accounts.

Even when the courts had decided that money was owed to the Utes, the Utes were not allowed control of the funds. Money owed to the tribe had to be appropriated by Congress and disbursed through the agency. It could not be spent by the tribe without government permission. Money paid to individual Indians (between 1919 and 1929, for example, Southern Utes received about $600 per family per year) was placed in special bank accounts, and permission from the appropriate government officer was required before any withdrawals could be made. In countless ways the federal government, following its official goal of making the Indians self-reliant, actually kept them in a state of wardship and dependence.

The Utes felt that the government attitude was irritating, demeaning, and unfair. Not only did they possess a proud tradition of independence, but a special provision of the 1896 law had granted citizenship to all adult male Utes who accepted allotments. As Chief Buckskin Charley said, "I am a citizen, and we are all citizens, all Americans." But in spite of the fact that Utes registered for army service during the First World War (though some refused) and bought Liberty Bonds, they were certainly not treated as responsible citizens by the Indian agent, who could, if he wished, ignore the desires of the people he was supposed to be helping. Even full citizenship, granted to all American Indians by Congress in 1924, did not immediately affect the special trust responsibility for land and many other forms of Indian property with which the Bureau of Indian Affairs had been charged by Congress.

The early years of the twentieth century were difficult for the Utes. Often there was not enough food, especially in the winter. Because of treaty obligations to help the Utes, and because they recognized that the Utes could not support themselves right away, government officials issued monthly rations of food. Rations consisted mostly of beef (although salt pork and beans were sometimes substituted) along with flour, baking powder, sugar, salt, and soap. The amount was large enough to keep the Utes from starving, but it was not an adequate diet. Some officials had the idea that the Indians might work harder on their farms if they were given shorter rations. Rations were reduced in 1913 and ended in 1931, but by the latter date Utes were receiving cash payments from the money owed to the tribe by the government.

Most of the Utes continued to hunt and gather wild foods to eke out their diet, but with the settlement of southwestern Colorado, game had grown scarce, and the old Ute hunting territory had been reduced sharply. Until 1912 it was officially illegal for Indians to leave the reservation without permission, and agents frowned on hunting trips when, as they thought,

Utes should be doing productive work on the reservations.

The Bureau of Indian Affairs' attempts to turn the Southern Utes into farmers, although they continued for more than fifty years, were only partly successful. The land allotments had been intended as small farms, but only a few Utes were willing to work on them. Instead, they sometimes went to live with relatives elsewhere, since Ute family loyalty was very close, extending strongly to persons who would be considered "distant relations" in the White kinship system. Everything, including food, was freely shared. In this way they got out from under the thumb of their local agent, at least for a time. The agents bitterly resented practices like these, and one went so far as to suggest that elderly Utes be confined in a home for the aged so that they could not move about so freely and share their rations with younger members of their families. Many Utes with allotments found that their Spanish-speaking neighbors, who were experienced small farmers, were willing to lease and farm the Ute allotments, giving a cash payment or a share of the crop in return.

At any given time between 1899 and 1921, well under half of the Utes with allotments were living on their land, and only a small fraction of these were actually farming. Some were successful; a Southern Ute fair was held annually after 1907, with prizes awarded by the Utes themselves for outstanding produce and stock. But there were serious problems.

Reservation land is arid and must be irrigated to produce crops. However, all the rivers flow through White-owned areas before entering Indian land, and many water diversions sharply reduced available water. The government at first failed to guard the prior claims of the Utes under Colorado water law, and the stage was set for troublesome water adjudications in later years.

Another problem involved the government's idea that the Indians should "reimburse" the agency for whatever tools, seed, or other goods were issued to them by working on the irrigation ditches or other agency labor projects. In the Ute view, these things were owed to them under the treaties as partial repayment for their lost lands, and to have to work for them was like paying for them twice.

Still another problem involved land inheritance. When an Indian with an allotment died, the land would go to his heirs, but the Ute kinship system was very different from the one recognized under United States law. Relatives were called by different terms, and adoption was frequent. Ownership became very complicated. In 1907 a new law allowed the sale of Indian lands in "heirship" status, or those owned by "noncompetent" Indians such as minors or those judged incapable of handling their own affairs. Beginning in 1911, the agency superintendent followed a policy of selling allotments in outlying areas and concentrating Indian-owned land along the Los Pinos River and Spring Creek. Many of the White "guardians" appointed to make these sales for the Utes were agency employees and may have accepted their tasks willingly, with an eye to making some advantageous real estate transactions. By 1921, when the twenty-five year allotment period ended and the remaining allotments became the private property of their Indian owners, about 23,000 acres, or one-third of the allotments, had already been sold, almost all to Whites. With the permission of the Bureau of Indian Affairs, which still exercised trust responsibility over the land for the United States, individual owners continued to sell their land after 1921.

Meanwhile, many Utes took part-time jobs in nearby towns, usually as domestic and hotel workers, mechanics, etc. Employers were pleased with their work and wanted them back. But since it was government policy to make Utes into farmers, this development was discouraged by the agent.

At Ute Mountain the story was different. The Weminuches had rejected the idea of assimilation by going west. They had moved to a desert and mountain area where there was almost no arable soil, and they were determined to keep their accustomed ways of life, hunting and living in pole shelters or tepees and tending their beloved herds of horses. Some also acquired sheep and goats, as did their Navajo neighbors, and a few cattle, and at times a government herdsman was assigned to advise them. However, the chief problem for the Weminuches was the lack of an adequate water supply on the lower desert lands that formed their winter range. Their reservation headquarters was also located here. The government did not provide a satisfactory water supply on a permanent basis for several decades, even though promises had been made. Much of the Ute Mountain range was leased to White stockmen by the superintendent.

Almost all early Indian agents made some attempt to provide education for Ute children, but they met with firm opposition from Ute parents, who originally regarded White education as a waste of time at best and a serious danger to their children at worst. Events seemed to prove that Ute fears were justified.

Several types of education became available to Indians in the United States in the late nineteenth and early twentieth centuries, and each was tried at least once on the Ute reservations. All methods had some elements in common: all instruction was in English, with use of the native language being severely discouraged, often by strict punishments. Children were expected to learn the White ways of doing things and were taught that Indian ways were old, primitive, and disappearing; things to be ashamed of. Schools actively tried to counteract the influences of Indian families on their children.

The first type of school provided for the Utes was the agency day school. Children lived at home and were expected to attend school each day. Only children living near the agency could attend, and among the Utes in the earlier years day schools failed miserably. Registration figures might look good on paper, but daily attendance was quite another story. Agents often had to use rewards and threats to get any children at all to attend. In spite of many attempts to get a day school started, the comment could truthfully be made in 1900 that there had been virtually "no school heretofore." The Allen day school, near Bayfield met with some success among the Utes beginning in 1909.

The second type of school provided by the federal government was the boarding school, where Indian children lived in dormitories. Officials thought that these schools were excellent because the children could be removed from the influence of their families and tribes and could be more easily forced into the desired mold. Isolated from their loved ones and facing cruel punishments whenever they showed their Indianness, the children all too often sickened and died or escaped and tried to walk home over impossibly long distances. Appropriations for Indian schools were very meager, reflected in inadequate food and heat, in dreary quarters and uniforms, in a lack of books and other teaching materials, and in teachers who sometimes had substandard educations, who went elsewhere as soon as they could, and who often had little love for the children. The Utes had their share of bad experiences with boarding schools. In 1883 twenty-seven Ute children were sent to

Grand Junction Indian School football team.
*Courtesy Denver Public Library, Western History
Department.*

Grand Junction Indian School printing office.
Courtesy Denver Public Library, Western History Department.

Fort Lewis Indian School band. *Courtesy State Historical Society of Colorado.*

school in Albuquerque, and before they were allowed to come home, about half of them had died. An attempt to build a boarding school on the reservation in 1886 was foiled by a measles epidemic, followed by the collapse of the building four years after its construction. Of sixteen Ute children sent to the new Fort Lewis boarding school in 1892, two died and three became blind.

The Southern Ute boarding school was founded in Ignacio in 1902 and operated until it was closed by the Indian commissioner in 1920. Students from the Ignacio area were accepted on a "day school" basis; Southern Ute parents gradually overcame their well-founded fears of school when one was located in their own community, and by around 1912, almost all Southern Ute children were in school. Many of the children who attended Southern Ute Boarding School, however, were not Utes and came from outside Colorado. Children from the Navajo reservation were the most numerous.

This was also true of the other boarding schools in Colorado. The Fort Lewis Indian training school and Teller Institute, or Grand Junction Indian School (founded originally in 1886 for Utes from Utah), served Indians from a wide area of the United States, but in 1910 and 1911 the schools were transferred to the State of Colorado. In the case of Fort Lewis, the transfer agreement included a special provision that, in return for the school and about 6000 acres of land at Hesperus, the state would always provide free education for Indians at the school. The later history of that agreement will be discussed subsequently in this book. In 1915 a new boarding school was built for the Ute Mountain Utes at Towaoc, but most children on the western reservation did not attend school until much later.

Mission schools were operated by various churches on many Indian reservations and received some government encouragement. A Presbyterian school was begun in Ignacio by the Reverend A. J. Rodriguez in 1894 and had several Ute students during the years the agency lacked a school.

Indians also attended public schools sponsored by states and localities. In some of these, efforts were made specifically to educate Indians, but in most cases Indian children simply found themselves a minority in classrooms among non-Indians. They had to adjust on their own, and were usually thought by their teachers to be very quiet youngsters. Some public schools refused to take Indian students because Indians did not pay local or state taxes in support of the schools. At various times the Ignacio public school took this attitude, but by 1920 most young Southern Ute children attended the public school.

A pattern of school attendance typical for many American Indians was found also among the Utes. They remained in school with considerable success through the fourth grade, but in the fifth grade they began to drop out. Few Utes actually completed elementary school, and as late as the early 1930s only a tiny percentage of Utes had enrolled in high school or college. Some reasons for this may be that individual competition, which is strongly encouraged by the American system of education, is discouraged by Ute culture, which values group loyalty, or that Ute children felt anti-Indian prejudice directed against them. They also may have resented the harsh discipline and separation from their families, or may have felt that the things they were taught would not be of future value.

Prior to the 1950s, the Bureau of Indian Affairs was charged with the responsibility for Indian health, but problems were manifold. Congressional appropriations in this area were miserable. At most times the attention of an agency physician or nurse was provided, but not all Utes could avail themselves of such services even if they wished to do so because of the vast size of the reservations. For a period around 1905, the only White medical care for the Ute Mountain Utes was provided by a druggist in Cortez. Hospitals were built on both reservations, but Utes were very slow to use them because their traditions taught them that places in which people have died should be avoided. Although they tended to feel that White doctors could treat some ailments successfully, other problems were considered to be the province of the traditional Ute healer, the medicine man. In recent years medical science has come to realize that these medicine men possessed valuable knowledge of healing herbs and the role of the mind in curing the body. The record of government-related Indian health services was not encouraging from any standpoint. Reservation Indians have had the worst health records, the highest infant mortality, and the lowest life expectancy of any group in the American population throughout the twentieth century. These factors were reflected in the decreasing population of the Utes. The Southern Utes had 428 people in 1890, but by 1920 they had declined to 334. A similar decline, from 530 in 1890 to

437 in 1925, was observed for the Ute Mountain Utes. If these figures seem to support the idea of the "disappearing Indian," it should be noted that the Utes began to increase again in the 1920s and have now reached about 800 among the Southern Utes and 1200 among the Ute Mountain Utes.

When the reservations were established, most Utes were living in tepees and brush shelters. The Bureau of Indian Affairs built a few houses in the 1880s, but at first these were used only for storage. Here again, the Utes felt that a place in which someone has died should be abandoned. Consequently, they were reluctant to live in permanent houses. Even today many structurally sound houses stand boarded up and empty on the Ute Mountain reservation for this reason. The Southern Utes overcame this feeling first, and by 1920 well over half of them lived in houses, especially during cold weather. But at Ute Mountain there were very few houses even then.

Many non-Indians do not realize how strongly most Indians want to remain Indian. The history of the reservations demonstrates the persistence of this desire; Indians have always wanted to live in the way identified by themselves as the Indian way. An incident which occurred in 1906 among the White River Utes, who had been removed from Colorado to Utah twenty-five years before, serves as an illustration. At that time, the Uintah-Ouray reservation had just been allotted, and much of the land was taken for non-Indian use. Two Ute chiefs, Red Cap and Mosisco, led some of their people away from the reservation to seek a place where they could live by themselves in their traditional way. They had heard that this was possible among their fellow Indians, the Sioux. They crossed Wyoming, causing a flurry of alarm among White people there, but kept away from settlements and did no more damage than to kill game animals and a very few cattle and sheep. Disappointment met them in South Dakota, where they found the situation of the Sioux to be as bad as their own. The United States Army took them "under protection," but the Indian Rights Association refused to support the Utes' actions. Nevertheless, the Utes were finally given the option of taking a little land on the Cheyenne River Sioux reservation. In little more than a year they asked to be returned to Utah.

An important sign of Ute survival is the Ute language, still spoken after almost 100 years of attempts to wipe it out. It is true that some Ute parents refused to teach it to their children because they thought it would handicap them in the larger world. But others, especially on the Ute Mountain reservation, have kept it alive. Among them, the Ute language continues to be a source of pride and cultural preservation.

Other Indian customs, such as social dances held periodically (including round dances and war dances which show the ability of the dancers) and traditional hand guessing games used for a bit of gambling, are kept alive not for show, or as a tourist attraction, but because the people themselves enjoy them. The Bear Dance, to give one example, has continued from year to year as an expression of Ute traditions. Some of the handcrafts, such as leatherwork, beadwork, basketry, and embroidery, managed to survive narrowly until interest was revived.

Indian identity is closely connected to Indian religion, and some of the most notable movements toward traditionalism or Indianism among the Utes have had an important religious expression. In the late nineteenth century, a movement of belief in world renewal, usually called the "Ghost Dance," began among the Paiutes of Nevada, the western relatives of the Utes. According to the new doctrine, if Indians would return to the old ways, wear symbolic costumes, and dance in circular patterns to sacred songs, the earth would heal herself. The forests, buffalos, and all the former richness of nature would return, and White people would be swept away. Indians would have the life that had been theirs before the strangers had come. This movement spread rapidly and widely to many tribes. The Utes were among the first to hear of it, and some of them adopted the dances and songs. However, the messenger who first brought the Ghost Dance to the Utes had set a date for the renewal of the world, and that day passed without incident. Ute visitors to the Paiutes brought back discouraging reports. Finally, in 1890 word came that scores of Sioux Ghost Dancers, promised by their leaders that bullets could not harm them, had been shot down by soldiers at the first Wounded Knee incident in South Dakota. After that, the Ghost Dance survived only in a few songs and prayers, but the great longing to which it had given expression continued.

Reservation days did see the revival of a great traditional observance that had taken shape on the Great Plains: the Sun Dance, in which the Utes still continue to seek a true orientation within the universe and a source of personal and tribal power. The Ute form of the Sun Dance is a dignified and awesome ceremony that demands much endurance from the dancers. There is no piercing of the flesh, but for four days and nights, without food or drink, the dancers stay in a circular enclosure open to the east and dance facing a central pole, a huge cottonwood trunk, forked at the top and decorated with paint, colored scarves, and a huge buffalo skull. Each dancer, wearing a special kilt and blowing on a bone whistle, moves along a path directly toward the pole, forward and backward, to music made by drummers and singers. At times during the long days healing ceremonies are held. It may happen that one or more dancers will receive special visions or infusions of power. The Sun Dance makes a deep impression on anyone who sees it and appreciates its serious purpose.

In the early years of the twentieth century another Indian religion, the Native American Church, gained many followers among the Utes, especially at Ute Mountain. The Native American Church is not limited to specific tribes, but has continued to grow rapidly among almost all tribes. Meetings are usually held around a fire in a tepee by a relatively small group. They last most of the night, with songs and prayers being accompanied by water-drums, rattles, and waving feather fans. Although the service is completely Indian, it can include Christian words and prayers. The sacrament of the Native American Church consists of eating the buds of the peyote cactus, which contains chemicals that may induce visions. This part of the ceremony is misunderstood by many non-Indians. Peyote is eaten in a carefully controlled setting and in relatively small amounts; it is not an indulgence, nor is it habit forming. The Native American Church forbids its members to indulge in alcohol or drugs; they are instead encouraged to work hard and take good care of their families. The religion has helped many Indians make successful adjustments to the difficult demands of the modern world.

Those who favored Indian assimilation into the general culture of the United States were very much opposed to the practice of Indian religions. In spite of the very clear guarantees of religious freedom in the Bill of Rights, a criminal code approved in 1884 and extended in various forms until 1933 prohibited the exercise of Indian religious ceremonies. Of course, not all observances were stopped, but some were held in secret. On the large Ute reservations this could be done.

The Indian Rights Association led a crusade against the use of peyote. Although peyote was never specifically outlawed on the federal level, it was made illegal by action of the legislatures in most western states. Colorado prohibited the possession and consumption of peyote from 1917 until 1967, when the law was declared an unconstitutional infringement on religious rights.

Many Utes are Christians, but not all think that Christianity is incompatible with Indian traditions and religious practices. Through the years most Ute Christians have customarily been Roman Catholics, because the Spanish New Mexicans have been their neighbors for centuries. Catholic priests have ministered to people on the reservation at various times. Several Protestant groups, including the Presbyterians and Southern Baptists, have sent missionaries as well. A Presbyterian church in Towaoc and both Protestant and Catholic churches in Ignacio have some Ute members.

The Southern Utes were far from isolated on their reservation. The town of Ignacio grew up in their midst, not ever a large town, but in its tricultural composition—Indian, Spanish, and "Anglo"—more similar to small communities in rural New Mexico than to most Colorado towns. Here the Spanish New Mexicans, experienced subsistence farmers and stock raisers for generations, were augmented by miners from northern Mexico (who brought the name "Durango" with them). Their fiestas, horse races, and wine shops were already familiar to Utes who visited towns just across the New Mexico line. The New Mexicans planned a new town near the site of Ignacio as early as 1907. But the actual founding of Ignacio in 1909 was the work of two Anglos. A store, bank, and hotel soon appeared, and the town was incorporated in 1913. The Utes learned much from their neighbors, especially the Spanish-speaking ones, and made common cause with them on occasion. Indians of other tribes were also close neighbors. The Navajos, whose lands border the Ute Mountain reservation, have lived in that section of Colorado for generations, building hogans and tending herds of sheep and goats. The Jicarilla Apaches and Paiutes have old ties of friendship and intermarriage with the Utes, as do some of the Pueblo Indians. For example, Luiz Ortiz, a Taos Indian, took one of the allotments in 1895. At least one Black had an important role in Southern Ute history. John Taylor, a Civil War veteran, married a Ute woman and received the allotment on which Ignacio was later built.

The Ute Mountain Utes were relatively more isolated, but still had neighbors—not all of them good. An incident occurred in 1914-15 which demonstrates how long the Indian removal sentiment persisted, and how hard some of the old anti-Indian frontier attitudes died. Some of the Weminuches, in their move to the west, had crossed the Utah line and occupied the San Juan country. After the removal of the Northern Utes, this land was proposed several times as a reservation for all Utes remaining in Colorado. Among the Utes who lived in Allen Canyon near Blanding, Utah, were Mancos Jim, Polk Narraguinnep, Johnny Benow, and Posey. Polk had a son named Tsenegat, or "Cry Baby." (He called *himself* Tsequit, or "Man Who Never Cries.") Tsenegat was indicted by a United States grand jury in Denver on a charge of murdering Juan Chacon, a sheepherder, on the Ute Mountain reservation. A United States marshal and a posse of deputized cowboys set out to make the arrest, but instead attacked without provocation or warning the Ute camp where Tsenegat was staying. Several people were killed, and in the fight Tsenegat escaped. Another anachronistic "Indian War" seemed to be underway. Headlines screamed, and Anglos on the Colorado-Utah border, seeing a chance to get rid of their Indian neighbors, herded the 160 or so "Blanding Utes" out of Utah and into the Ute Mountain reservation. The move was illegal, but the Utes had no recourse at the time. Polk, Posey, and Tsenegat had been hiding out near Navajo Mountain, but surrendered to General Hugh L. Scott, who parleyed with them without any military escort. Tsenegat was taken to Denver, tried, and found innocent. His defense was aided by the Indian Rights Association and J. W. Kershaw, a Menominee Indian lawyer. After several years the Allen Canyon Utes gradually returned to their lands in Utah, which are now regarded as a detached part of the Ute Mountain reservation.

A new wave of reform broke upon Indian country in the late 1920s and early 1930s. In 1924 Indians had been made citizens by an act of Congress and thereby given the protection of the Bill of Rights. In 1928 the Secretary of the Interior authorized the first impartial, independent study of Indian affairs in the twentieth century. The Brookings Institution, supported by Rockefeller money, appointed Lewis Meriam and a capable staff including Indian members such as Henry Roe

Cloud, a Winnebago, to carry out the investigation. The result, the Meriam Report, prompted a full-scale Senate inquiry into Indian affairs. The investigators found that the allotment policy had failed; it had reduced Indian lands (almost two-thirds of all remaining Indian land had been lost in a forty-year period—100 million acres out of 150 million) without making many Indians self-supporting. The government had failed to fulfill its responsibility toward Indians. Indian health was poor, and poverty and discontent were widespread. The Meriam Report was particularly critical of Indian education as represented by the boarding schools, which interfered with family life and failed to prepare children for the conditions they would meet after leaving school.

President Herbert Hoover began a laudable attempt to find more highly qualified people for staff positions in the Bureau of Indian Affairs when he appointed Charles J. Rhoads, the president of the Indian Rights Association, as B.I.A. commissioner. But the most far-reaching reforms occurred under John Collier, the intelligent social scientist who was appointed Commissioner of Indian Affairs by President Franklin D. Roosevelt in 1933. Collier had actively helped the Pueblo Indians organize against threats to their land. Like others of a new, more understanding group of Indians' friends, he was convinced that in a democracy different cultural groups should be able to keep their own identities and ways of life. Instead of "assimilation," Collier believed that Indian tribes should be encouraged to run their own affairs and make their own valuable contributions to a pluralistic society. As a step in this direction he said,

> No interference with Indian religious life or expression will hereafter be tolerated. The cultural history of Indians is in all respects to be considered equal to that of any non-Indian group. And it is desirable that Indians be bilingual —fluent and literate in the English language, and fluent in their vital, beautiful and efficient native languages. The Indian arts are to be prized, nourished and honored.[1]

The Bureau of Indian Affairs' new guarantee of religious freedom for Indians was confirmed by congressional action and made definitive by the extension of the Bill of Rights to Indians. Collier appointed many Indians to positions in the Bureau of Indian Affairs. Under Collier's leadership, Congress passed the Indian Reorganization Act in 1934. This act stopped new allotments and extended the government's trust protection over Indian land for an indefinite period. It authorized the purchase of land for Indian tribes; allowed tribes to organize their own official tribal governments by vote, with some decision-making powers on the reservations; and authorized Indians to form tribal corporations for the management of funds and property.

Members of the Southern Ute Tribal Council, 1959–60. Seated, Chairman John E. Baker; standing, left to right, Sunshine Smith, Anna Marie Scott, Anthony Burch, Bonny Kent, Clifford Baker. *Courtesy State Historical Society of Colorado.*

Under this act, the Southern Ute tribe wrote and ratified a constitution in 1936. The governing body created by that constitution is a tribal council of six members, two of whom are elected each year. A chairman had been formerly selected from the council itself, but a 1975 amendment provided that the chairman be directly elected. The first tribal chairman was the last hereditary chief, Antonio Buck, Sr., the son of Buckskin Charley, who had died the same year.

The Ute Mountain tribe was similarly organized in 1940, with a tribal council of seven members, one of whom is elected annually by the Allen Canyon (Utah) community.

Through the tribal councils, the Utes govern themselves democratically. The councils have established offices and committees to deal with the various aspects of tribal business, such as public relations, law and order (tribal police), property and supply, fish and game, maintenance, extension, agricultural resources, family planning, tribal membership, and health, education, and welfare. Tribal courts have been organized to deal with offenses under their own jurisdiction. From the time tribal governments were organized, their ability to make effective decisions has increased. Approval by the Department of the Interior is still required for most tribal council decisions, and the Bureau of Indian Affairs still retains trust responsibility over much land and natural resource use and development. The Indian Reorganization Act was a step in the direction of self-government for Indians; it was not a declaration of independence, nor a relinquishment of the trust responsibility vested in the federal government.

In 1937 a large amount of federal land was returned to the Utes. The tract had once been reservation land, but had been thrown open to non-Indian settlement as "surplus" land (according to the provisions of the Dawes Act). However, because the land had never been homesteaded, about 220,000 acres were restored to the Southern Utes. The land, scattered in a wild, crazy-quilt pattern among the allotments and privately owned tracts, was best suited to grazing and lumbering. Practically all the farmland had been settled long before. At about the same time, the Ute Mountain Utes had 30,000 acres restored to their tribal patrimony. Gas and oil leases on the tribal land added to the Utes' income.

The depression years were hard for everyone in America, but the Utes had been living in what amounted to depression conditions since the reservation had been created. Emergency conservation work connected with the Civilian Conservation Corps in the 1930s provided jobs and leadership experience for Utes in more than 100 projects. The Works Progress Administration sponsored the construction of a memorial to four great chiefs—Ouray, Ignacio, Buckskin Charley, and Severo—in the Ute tribal park near Ignacio.

During the Second World War, many young Ute men served in the United States armed forces and gained additional experience and training. Many became leaders in the tribal government when they returned. It should be noted that Ute women have also given valuable leadership in tribal offices, including membership on the tribal council.

The war effort drained funds from Indian projects. Due to a lack of water, the subagency at Towaoc, with the school and hospital, was closed for several years. But a welcome source of financial resources appeared in the 1950s. A new case before the United States Court of Claims, asking payment for lands taken from them, had been opened in 1938 by the Colorado and Utah Utes. In 1950 an award was finally granted which included about $12 million for the two Colorado tribes. The payment did not come in the form of a check; a plan was needed to indicate how funds would be spent, plus Congress had to appropriate the money.

At this point the Utes took an important step forward in self-determination. Rejecting the attempt of the B.I.A. superintendent's staff to prepare a plan for them, the two tribal councils appointed planning committees to design a rehabilitation plan. The plan was to originally be for both reservations, but separate approval was eventually given to Southern Ute and Ute Mountain. The Ute Rehabilitation Plan was a comprehensive program intended to help the Utes develop in the following areas: family and community life, education, health, financial credit, land improvement, housing and utilities, agriculture, grazing, irrigation, timber, roads, private enterprise, and tribal business. This balanced plan, in operation since the mid-1950s, has shown solid results in almost all areas of concern on the Southern Ute reservation. Ute Mountain's progress has been substantial, although less visible, but needs there are very much in evidence.

Over the past twenty years, reservation life has changed greatly. The last few federal administrations have had official policies of giving tribal councils a greater degree of self-determination. True enough, a big scare in the mid-1950s made it appear that the government wanted to cut the Indians "free" from federal supervision and federal aid at the same time. If Indian tribes are to make the transition to self-determination, they will need to receive the resources necessary to make the change; attempts at sudden "termination" have been marked failures. Fortunately, during the 1960s Indian tribes received federal aid for community development under the Office of Economic Opportunity and the Economic Development Administration. The funds were put to good use, and many

Pino Nuche Motel at Ignacio, Southern Ute Reservation. *Courtesy State Historical Society of Colorado.*

Indians gained experience in applying for grants and administering federal programs. The tribal governments and the Bureau of Indian Affairs are by far the most important sources of jobs on the reservations today.

Agriculture and grazing continue to be important economic factors on the reservations, but they involve only a small segment of the Utes. Other areas of economic development are not being neglected. The Ute Mountain Utes have a cooperative ceramics factory at Towaoc that produces beautiful modern pottery based on traditional Indian designs. At Ignacio the Southern Utes have built the Pino Nuche Motel Pu-ra-sa, complete with swimming pool, restaurant, and gift shop which sells locally made Ute Indian arts and crafts. This tourist facility is next to the tribal community center, which includes meeting rooms, classrooms, recreational facilities, and another swimming pool.

Indian health services were transferred from the Bureau of Indian Affairs to the United States Public Health Service in 1955. The level of appropriations has remained below what is needed, in view of the fact that Indian rates of hospitalization are still well above the national average. Alcoholism is a serious health problem for many Indians, as it is among the population at large. Most cases that come before Ute tribal courts involve drinking. Accidents and injuries, often alcohol-related, are leading causes of death. The sale of alcohol on Indian reservations was illegal until the 1950s and contributed to the "problem drinker" syndrome; however, the situation seems to be improving. The problem is receiving much attention. An

99

Southern Utes, early 1970s. *Courtesy State Historical Society of Colorado.*

alcoholic rehabilitation center at Towaoc does valuable work.

Housing has greatly improved in recent years; building has assured that most Southern Utes have a safe water supply and live in houses comparable to those of their non-Indian neighbors. A new housing project is under way at Towaoc as well, where chronic water shortage is still a problem.

Education for the Utes has moved almost entirely to the public realm. The Southern Ute boarding school was reopened in 1930, mainly for Navajo children, although many Utes attended. Southern Ute High School was added in 1943. The possibilities for integrated public education were greatly improved by the Johnson-O'Malley Act, passed by Congress with John Collier's warm support. The federal government was given the right to contract with local school districts for Indian education and to compensate them with funds for that purpose. In 1956 the Southern Ute schools were merged with the Ignacio public schools. Indian children have their share, or more than their share, of the costs of education paid with federal funds to the school district. The boarding school dormitories still provide accommodations for Indian children from outside the Ignacio area. The majority of other Ute children now attend public schools in Cortez, Durango, and Bayfield under similar arrangements. The Ute education level is rapidly approaching the national average. A federal grant now supports a learning center at the Southern Ute tribal headquarters near Ignacio. Both the learning center and the tribal youth camp are open to all children in the area.

By gaining control over their own lives and improving their physical well-being, Utes are renewing pride in their own heritage. Classes are being held in the Ute language for young people who have not learned to speak Ute. Colorado's new laws supporting multicultural and multilingual education among large, culturally diverse minorities will probably encourage this development in La Plata and Montezuma counties. Steps are being taken to produce a standard written and printed form of the Ute language which could be used on ballots (as the Voting Rights Law of 1975 apparently requires) and in bilingual books which could bring Ute history and stories to classrooms.

Future plans for both tribes include preservation and dissemination of knowledge about Indian heritage. A heritage center with opportunities to see "living history" is planned at Ignacio. The Ute Mountain Utes are planning to open a series of interesting cliff dwellings in a canyon just south of Mesa Verde National Park, and a visitor center will include information on Ute history. Hopefully these centers will explain to visitors that being Indian belongs not only to the past, but also continues into the present and the future. Indians, proud of their past and open to what is valuable in the present, continue to define for themselves what it means to be Indian.

In the future Utes should attain greater control over their own community so that they can chart their own direction.

Southern Utes, early 1970s. *Courtesy State Historical Society of Colorado.*

Indians in the Cities

Indians have always lived in Denver, from the 1850s when Little Raven and his Arapahoes camped with the new settlers along the South Platte, through the 1870s, when Utes such as Kaneache, Colorow, and Piah made frequent visits to the Denver agency and even held the Bear Dance in the city.

Colorful visitors, like the Apaches who camped in City Park in 1900, also aroused citizen interest. But other Indians simply settled down in the city, adjusted to city life, and caused very little comment. Their homes, dress, and employment were little different from those of their neighbors. In most cases, however, they kept close ties to family members back on the reservations and returned periodically for visits. Indians who had been given allotments under the Dawes Act of 1887 and who had lost their land, either by sale or by various legal arrangements, often moved to the cities.

The Meriam Report of 1928 noted that considerable numbers of tribal Indians had moved to cities. Most were seeking better jobs and living conditions; some had experienced difficulties with federal officials and policies on the reservations. The report said that, in general, they were "resourceful, energetic and better educated" than other Indians.[1] During this period the Bureau of Indian Affairs did not follow them to provide any special services. In the city they were as much on their own as anyone else.

Many Indians served in the armed forces during World War II. They were stationed all around the world and often received awards for distinctive service. Indian languages, and Navajo in particular, were used as coding systems; two Navajos relaying messages over the radio in Navajo were absolutely incomprehensible to Germans or Japanese. The war years gave many young Indians a taste of city life and took them away from the reservations. Some stayed in the cities after the war. Indian veterans of Korea and Viet Nam experienced much the same thing.

By the late 1940s, enough Indians were living in the city

to excite the interest of the newspapers and the concern of welfare agencies. In 1949 the Bureau of Indian Affairs, burdened with a rapidly increasing population on the reservations and pushed by political cries to get itself "out of the Indian business," began a program for off-reservations placement. This was done as a pilot project among the Navajos, and Denver was one of the first cities chosen for relocation. It was a voluntary program; Indians applied on the reservation and, if accepted, were given transportation, vocational training, housing, expense money, and assistance in finding jobs for a period of time, with the expectation that they would become self-supporting. Pleased with what seemed to be early success, the B.I.A. made the Indian relocation program a nationwide policy in the early 1950s. Primarily to aid the relocation, or employment assistance activities in the Denver area, the Bureau of Indian Affairs located an office in the city in 1954.

The increase in Indians living in cities during the 1950s was phenomenal. In the West the growth in numbers of "urban Indians" has been estimated at over 200 percent from 1950 to 1960. Although reliable figures are hard to obtain, there is no doubt that Indian migrants to the cities were very numerous. In the same period, 30,000 Indians were assisted to relocate by the B.I.A., and 1,600 heads of families were vocationally trained. The program continued its rapid expansion, with 20,000 receiving vocational training between 1960 and 1968. In the Denver Field Employment Assistance Office alone, about 1,800 persons received vocational training in 1962–73, and of these, slightly more than half completed the program. A much larger number of Indians, probably several times that indicated by the figures given above, moved to cities on their own without B.I.A. assistance.

Many did not stay. In fact, one sociological study determined that half of all Navajos who came to Denver returned to the reservation within six months.[2] The picture is complicated by the fact that most Indians retain very close ties with their friends and relatives "back home." Even if they have lived in the city for many years, they still retain their tribal identity. The B.I.A. began to reduce the relocation program in the early 1970s, concentrating instead on job development in and near the reservations.

Most of the new urban Indians in Colorado came to the Denver-Boulder metropolitan region; Colorado Springs also has a sizable Indian population. Smaller groups of Indians now populate most other Colorado cities. Although Indians relocated in Denver were usually given apartments in the Capitol Hill district, they soon moved to all areas of the city, including the suburbs. The B.I.A. helped those on relocation with down payments for houses. In Denver no "urban Indian ghetto" has been created. In fact, the Indian population has not even concentrated itself in one section of the city. Not all Indians who left the reservations went to large cities; some also became seasonal migrant workers in agricultural regions. Sioux, for example, helped in the potato harvests of northeastern Colorado.

Most urban Indians, like many of their White neighbors who came to Colorado during the same period, were from other states. Very few Utes took part in relocation. The tribes with the largest urban populations in Colorado today are the Navajo and Sioux. However, most tribes of the United States, including those of Alaska, are represented in the front range cities by large or small groups—or perhaps by only one person (as is the case for some of the smaller tribes). The Indian population of Colorado increased rapidly during the last two decades. Between 1960 and 1970 the official census figures more than doubled from over 4000 to over 8000, but the census probably failed to count many Indians as Indians. A reasonable estimate for 1975 might be 8500 in the Denver-Boulder area, 2000 reservation Utes in southwestern Colorado, and 1500 Indians in the rest of the state, or a total of about 12,000.

Those who migrated to the cities faced many obstacles. Most Indians came from small, closely knit rural communities and had never lived in large cities. They suffered from loneliness and "cultural shock." Jobs were difficult to find, and Indians sometimes discovered that their vocational training had not qualified them for the jobs that were most available. Wages for the unskilled work that many of them had to do at first were low, often lower than they had received on the reservation. Many services available to Indians on the reservation were not offered in the city; the Indian Health Service, for example, did not ordinarily serve urban Indians unless they returned to the reservation. Indians were also unfamiliar with the processes involved in applying for city and state services. Local officials, who mistakenly thought Indians to be "wards of the federal government" and therefore ineligible for nonfederal services, were often unwilling to help Indians. Actually, Indians are as eligible for state and local services as other citizens. For many Indians the city was confusing, cold, and frightening. Many could not speak English well. In such circumstances it was not surprising that some turned to alcohol. The arrest record of Indians in the cities for all offenses, and especially for alcohol-related offenses, has shown a rate several times higher than that for any other ethnic group. Of course, many Indians made the transition to urban life with few difficulties and were soon working as teachers, government administrators, construction foremen, social workers, and in almost every other kind of job. Many are widely known and respected among Indian people and non-Indians alike.

Concerned Indians soon saw the need for organizations to help new urban Indian residents. They needed advice and education on how to cope with the city from the point of view of those who had already learned to do so. They needed a social organization to provide the community life they were missing. They also needed someone they could turn to in times of personal crisis.

The first Indian organization in Denver, begun in 1955, was the White Buffalo Council. It is dedicated to assisting Indian people in adjusting to a new life in the city, while

White Buffalo Council pow wow. *Courtesy Denver Public Library, Western History Department.*

106

encouraging the traditional values and cultural heritage of all Indian people. Arts and crafts classes, classes in Indian dancing, sports programs, and emergency assistance are important activities. The White Buffalo Council holds weekly dinners followed by Indian dancing, and monthly and annual pow wows. By 1960 it had grown to a membership of 300, representing eighteen different tribes. A social organization in Colorado Springs, the Pike's Peak Intertribal Indian Club, also holds annual pow wows. Groups of skilled singers and drummers, like the Denver Indian Singers, provide music at pow wows and other social events, and some have produced their own record albums.

In 1971 Denver Native Americans United opened the Denver Indian Center in a former synagogue at the corner of 16th Avenue and Gaylord Street. D.N.A.U., a consortium of about fifteen local Indian organizations, provides at the Indian Center traditional and modern activities such as cultural, educational, and recreational programs, emergency assistance, and social services.

Two of the Indian Center's member organizations concern alcoholism and drug problems. The Tepee Alcoholism Center, founded as a family-oriented agency administered by Denver Opportunity, is concerned with the individual, the family, and the community in relation to alcohol and drug abuse problems. The services include counseling, crisis intervention, Alcoholics Anonymous, group discussions, and referral services to treatment-related programs. Eagle Lodge is a nonprofit organization engaged in the rehabilitation of those with alcohol or drug problems. Services include counseling, therapy, education and recreation, cultural orientation, and Alcoholics Anonymous for about twenty-five live-in clients.

The Indian Center and some of its constituent organizations were supported for a time by funds from the Office of Economic Opportunity and various programs of the Department of Health, Education and Welfare. During the "War on Poverty" days of the late 1960s and early 1970s, new sources of federal funds outside the B.I.A. became available for Indians in urban areas as well as for those on reservations. Indians became eligible for these programs on the same basis as other citizens, and some federal agencies set up "Indian desks" to answer questions concerning the special circumstances of Indians. To help coordinate the Indian-related activities of a sometimes bewildering number of government organizations, the B.I.A. set up a liaison office in Denver. A B.I.A. plant management branch was also located in Littleton during the early 1970s.

Religious groups have been ministering to Indians in Denver for many years. There are Indian churches with Indian pastors. Many denominations have initiated Indian work in the city, such as the Episcopal Diocesan Indian Committee with its family visitation program, and the De Smet Indian Center of the Catholics. It should be noted that, on a national level, most major denominations no longer treat Indians as the objects of missionary activity, but have placed their Indian work under boards composed of Indian members. The Native American Church is as active in urban areas as on the reservations and is quite strong in Denver.

All of the urban Indian activities mentioned above are pan-Indian, that is, they are open to and include Indians of many different tribes. In them, Indians are identified *as Indians*, in addition to their tribal origins. Indians increasingly feel a sense of unity with other Indians, especially in urban areas where they form a small, but very self-conscious, minority. This feeling is becoming stronger as a new generation of Indians grows up within the cities and intertribal marriages become more common. Pow wows are a pan-Indian institution. Indians of different tribes join in dances and dance contests which originated among a number of tribes. Costumes are eclectic, borrowing decorative elements from tribes around the country, although one cannot avoid the impression that the dominant note reflects Plains Indian culture. Indians generally have come to feel that they have more in common with Indians of other tribes than they do with other ethnic groups in America.

Indian children in the city are educated in public schools. Since Indian homes are scattered throughout Denver, there are not many Indians in any one school, so there are no bilingual or bicultural programs for them as yet. Today, more Indians are completing high school and attending college than in the past. Public school districts in Colorado that received grants from the Office of Indian Education in 1976 to develop and implement elementary and secondary school programs designed to meet the special needs of Indian children were located in Ignacio, Denver, Colorado Springs, Fort Collins, Longmont, and Naturita, and in the counties of Adams, Douglas, Dolores, and San Miguel.

The Colorado institution of higher education with the greatest number of Indians is Fort Lewis College. When the Indian school lands at Hesperus were transferred to state ownership in 1911, the State of Colorado agreed to provide education at that school free of tuition for Indian students. Fort Lewis then was an agricultural and vocational high school, but became Fort Lewis A. & M. College, a branch of Colorado A. & M. at Fort Collins, in 1933. In 1948 it became an independent college under the State Board of Agriculture and moved to a new campus on a mesa above Durango. Enrollment increased rapidly in the 1960s, and among the new students were many Indians, attracted by the free tuition, the presence of an Indian student community, and special intercultural classes and programs. Indian enrollment rose to over 200, about ten percent of the entire student body. The Colorado state legislature then decided that the state could no longer afford to offer free tuition to all Indians and in 1971 passed a law restricting the privilege to Indians who are residents of Colorado. However, both the United States District Court and the Tenth Circuit Court of Appeals declared this state law invalid. In 1975 the legislature passed a new law restoring free tuition for Indians attending Fort Lewis College.

Scholarships from tribal funds or from the B.I.A. are often available for qualified Indian students. However, these grants do not cover all expenses. United Scholarship Service, an organization with headquarters in Denver, has placed additional financial help in the hands of Indian students. Generally, Indian college students have had a high drop-out rate and have done better when in contact with an Indian counselor or with someone who has had specific experience with the situations faced by Indians.

Other colleges and universities in Colorado have Indian students, teachers, and special programs. An outstanding example is the University of Colorado at Boulder, attended by a large group of Indian students. The Department of Anthropology, with its former chairman, now Professor Emeritus Omer C. Stewart, has taken a strong interest in contemporary American Indian issues based on careful academic studies. Dr. Ruth Underhill, Professor Emeritus of Anthropology at the University of Denver, guided many of the salutary reforms of Indian education of the middle 1930s, as supervisor of Indian education. She has studied many tribes, including the Papagos and Navajos, and has written scores of books and articles of lasting value.

Museums and libraries, as well as colleges and universities, have operated as centers where Indians and non-Indians alike can become familiar with Indian heritage. The Denver Art Museum has one of the finest collections of Indian art in existence. Anyone who views only the small portion of the collection on display may sense the richness of American Indian cultures. Groups of Indian children are often brought to see the exhibits. The Denver Museum of Natural History also has a large collection of Indian materials, and excellently arranged exhibits in this field are being expanded rapidly. The Natural History Museum is assisted in its Indian displays by Patty Harjo, an Indian staff member, and an all-Indian advisory board, assuring an accurate and sensitive portrayal of Indian life. The Colorado State Historical Society specializes in museum, library, and photographic materials relating to the Indians of Colorado, and has created fascinating dioramas of early Indian activities. They maintain a Ute historical museum in Montrose on the site of Ouray's farm. In its extensive Western History Collection, the Denver Public Library has assembled research resources of unique value relating to American Indians. Colorado has become a major center for American Indian studies.

The Denver-Boulder area has more than local importance in Indian affairs by providing leaders for many national Indian movements. Located near the "center of gravity" of Indian country, and about equally accessible from the Plains, the Southwest, the Northwest, and Oklahoma, Denver and Boulder serve as headquarters for several Indian organizations and often provide the location for important national Indian meetings. In Denver one can keep in touch with the progress of Indian issues all around the country.

The National Congress of American Indians held its organizing convention in Denver in 1944. It was the first nationwide Indian organization in which Indians spoke and acted for themselves. Originally formed by representatives from tribes on reservations, N.C.A.I. later broadened its base to include a voice for urban resident Indians. Headquartered in Washington so that its staff could easily contact senators, representatives, and administration officials, N.C.A.I. became very active in protecting Indian land and water, voting rights, tax exemptions, hunting and fishing rights, education, health, and welfare. N.C.A.I. was responsible for securing the enactment of the Indian Claims Act, which allowed tribes to sue the United States government for treaty violations and redress of other grievances. The organization soon became involved in the crisis over the attempt to terminate federal responsibility for Indian tribes. For eight years during this difficult "termination" period, N.C.A.I. had as executive director the eloquent, capable Helen Peterson, an Oglala Sioux who had lived for some time in Colorado and had served on the Denver Commission on Human Rights. Much serious damage to Indian tribes was prevented by N.C.A.I.'s tireless and timely work in representing the Indian viewpoint.

The insistence of N.C.A.I. and others that Indian interests are best guarded and represented by knowledgeable Indians led to the appointment of Robert L. Bennett, an eminently qualified Oneida Indian, as Commissioner of Indian Affairs. His two successors are also Indians, and it appears that a new tradition has begun. The preferential appointment of Indians to jobs in the Bureau of Indian Affairs has withstood an attack in the courts.

American Indian Development, founded in 1956, sponsored six-week workshops with credit granted by the University of Colorado to teach young Indians the basic facts about Indian history and current affairs. A.I.D. believed that in order to defend their rights, Indians had to know what those rights were and how to work for desirable changes.

The Native American Rights Fund, an organization which provides legal counsel in cases involving important issues in Indian law, has its national headquarters in Boulder. Law is a crucial field for Indians today, since a huge body of special laws applies to Indians and since Indian rights are more often defended in the courts than anywhere else. The most articulate voice in this field is that of the author and lawyer, Vine Deloria, Jr., a Standing Rock Sioux with a law degree from the University of Colorado. Deloria has done much to increase awareness of the importance of educating Indians as lawyers. He resides in the Denver area, but is at home everywhere in Indian country. He was also executive director of N.C.A.I. His books, such as *Custer Died for Your Sins, Behind the Trail of Broken*

State Supreme Court hearing. *Courtesy Denver Public Library, Western History Department.*

Treaties, and *We Talk, You Listen,* are spiced with humor and sharp-edged accuracy.

Many other national Indian organizations were organized in the Denver area, such as the Coalition of Indian-Controlled School Boards, the Tribal Indian Land Rights Association, and Call of the Council Drums. Conferences on Indian issues, too numerous to list, were held in the city. To the Indian's ancient delight in well-phrased oratory and wisdom applied to shared concerns was added the ease of travel by automobile and airplane, and the sense that steps could be taken by Indians in unity and self-determination.

But the pace seemed too slow. Government officials tended to give speeches expressing agreement with Indian goals rather than to remove the blocks on the roads leading to those goals. In the early 1970s, a large number of Indians began to support more militant political action. At first this was done moderately, with considerable tact and humor.

The National Indian Youth Council provided educational workshops and sponsored action projects. A sit-in at the B.I.A. office in Littleton ended in a trial in which the demonstrators were declared innocent.

The American Indian Movement, founded in Minneapolis to intervene in arrests of Indians and provide meals and "survival training" for Indian children in the city, had a Denver chapter by 1971. A.I.M. in Denver had an admirable ability of choosing exactly those issues that seemed to compel non-Indians to see the Indian viewpoint. They protested such actions as the showing of a lurid motion picture which exploited a distorted image of Indians. (The theatre switched to another film.) They demonstrated against the indiscriminate excavation of Indian gravesites by amateurs and professionals using methods that could never be used legally in non-Indian cemeteries. They pointed out the implications of prejudice in the presence of questions on the state bar examination that referred to "Little Big Man and his squaw"—the term "squaw" is regarded as deeply offensive by most Indians—and the question was removed.

Those Indians who objected to A.I.M.'s stridency and methods of protest usually agreed that its goals were laudable, and that the publicity it brought to Indian problems might help increase public awareness.

These local events occurred in a climate of Indian activism across the nation. Beginning with a "fish-in" demonstration to protest the attempts of the State of Washington to deny Indians their fishing rights guaranteed by treaty, the movement continued through occupations of Alcatraz Island, the Bureau of Indian Affairs building in Washington, D. C., the historic town of Wounded Knee in South Dakota, and the Fairchild semiconductor plant at Farmington, New Mexico, all of which received wide coverage in the nation's news media and made virtually every American realize that all was not well in Indian country. At the same time, the actions of some Indians and the sometimes hasty overreaction of government officials produced situations of violence, property destruction, and some Indian and non-Indian deaths. Within the Indian communities, serious division of opinion developed concerning the direction of these events.

Although disagreements on methods and courses of action exist, most Indians agree on their broad objectives. Also, most agree that achievement of these goals will be sought better through political action rather than through violence.

Indians prize a sense of their own Indian identity. They want to take an important part in American life without losing what is distinctively their own. The days of "assimilation" on non-Indian terms are gone.

113

The future should see the control of Indian issues placed more firmly in Indian hands. As self-determination becomes a reality, Indians will continue to develop their own leadership. On reservations, laws now make it possible for the Bureau of Indian Affairs to contract with tribal governments for services formerly provided by the B.I.A. itself. This should become the rule rather than the exception. Tribes will move away from direct federal control without losing needed federal support.

An area of concern for Indians and non-Indians alike is the impact of the development of natural resources on Indian reservations. Widespread strip mining and pollution must be controlled to avoid serious deterioration of the land base of Indian tribes. Indians must win additional safeguards to protect their lands and community life.

In the next few years, non-Indians who want to be friends of Indians will have to understand that Indians are determined to make their own decisions. Indians are through being told what they must do by one non-Indian "expert" after another. Indians do not like to be put "on exhibit;" they are self-respecting human beings.

For those who understand this, friendship between Indians and non-Indians can be deep and mutually rewarding, with respect on both sides. Non-Indians should study Indian history. Colorado owes much to the American Indians. The land was once theirs, and they treated it with reverence and with an understanding of what is now called "ecology"—human dependence upon and balance with nature. They discovered the uses of animals and plants for food, medicine, clothing, shelter, and tools, developing a valuable ethnic science. Among their own people they knew how to live in peace and cooperation governed by consensus and a basic kind of democracy. Their traditions taught them generosity and a fulfilling life style which is not ruled by the clock. Non-Indians can continue to learn from Indians today, because Indian contributions are not limited to the past. They are intelligent and resourceful people who are alive in the present.

Notes

Chapter I
1. "Where the Columbines Grow."

Chapter III
1. Pedro de Castañeda, *Narrative of the Expedition of Coronado,* tr. by George Parker Winship, in Bureau of American Ethnology, 14th Annual Report (1893).

Chapter V
1. U.S. Constitution, Art. I, Sec. 2, Cl. 3. See also Art. I, Sec. 8, Cl. 3.
2. The Northwest Ordinance, Art. 3 (1787).
3. U.S. Constitution, Art. 2, Sec. 2, Cl. 2, and Art. 6, Cl. 2.
4. U.S. Supreme Court, *Cherokee vs. Georgia,* 5 Pet. 1 (1831), and *Worcester vs. Georgia,* 5 Pet. 515 (1832).
5. *Weekly Rocky Mountain News,* April 20, 1864, p. 2.
6. *Ibid.,* April 18, 1860, p. 2.
7. *Ibid.,* February 26, 1863, p. 2, and July 16, 1863, p. 2.
8. *Ibid.,* August 17, 1864, p. 1.
9. George E. Hyde, *Life of George Bent, Written from His Letters* (Norman: University of Oklahoma Press, 1968), p. 155.
10. Mari Sandoz, *Cheyenne Autumn* (New York: McGraw-Hill, 1953).
11. Henry M. Teller to Nathan C. Meeker, January 3, 1878, quoted in Marshall Sprague, *Massacre: The Tragedy at White River* (Boston: Little, Brown, 1957), 57–58.
12. Ross V. Miller, "Shawsheen: The Heroine of the Meeker Massacre." Denver: The Westerners, *The Brand Book* 7, No. 3. Note that Utes of this period are usually referred to in written sources by their Anglicized names, but are perhaps more properly called by their Ute names, for example: Tsashin (Susan), Nicaagat (Jack), Quinkent (Douglas), Canavish (Johnson), Sowowic (Sowerwick), etc.

Chapter VI
1. U.S. Commissioner of Indian Affairs, *Annual Report,* 1934, p. 90.

Chapter VII
1. Institute for Government Research, *The Problem of Indian Administration* (Baltimore: Johns Hopkins, 1928), 671.
2. Robert S. Weppner, "Urban Economic Opportunities: The Example of Denver," Chapter 6 in Jack O. Waddell and O. Michael Watson, eds., *The American Indian in Urban Society* (Boston: Little, Brown, 1971), 245–73.

Bibliography

Books:

Andrist, Ralph K. *The Long Death: The Last Days of the Plains Indians.* New York: Macmillan, 1964.

Bahr, Howard M., Bruce A. Chadwick, and Robert C. Day, eds. *Native Americans Today: Sociological Perspectives.* New York: Harper & Row, 1972.

Bakker, Elna and Richard G. Lillard. *The Great Southwest.* Palo Alto, California: American West, 1972.

Baldwin, Gordon C. *The Ancient Ones: Basketmakers and Cliff Dwellers of the Southwest.* New York: W. W. Norton, 1963.

Bean, Luther E. *Land of the Blue Sky People: A Story of the San Luis Valley.* Alamosa, Colorado: Ye Olde Print Shoppe, 1962.

Billard, Jules B. *The World of the American Indian.* Washington, D.C.: National Geographic Society, 1974.

Bluemel, Elinor. *One Hundred Years of Colorado Women.* Denver, Colorado: Bluemel, 1973.

Braidwood, Robert J. *Prehistoric Men.* 8th ed. Glenview, Illinois: Scott, Foresman, 1974.

Brandon, William. *The American Heritage Book of Indians.* Edited by Alvin M. Josephy. New York: Simon & Schuster, 1961.

Ceram, C. W. *The First American.* New York: Harcourt Brace Jovanovich, 1971.

Claiborne, Robert. *The First Americans.* New York: Time-Life Books, 1973.

Collier, John. *On the Gleaming Way: Navajos, Eastern Pueblos, Zunis, Apaches, and Their Land; and Their Meanings to the World.* 2nd ed. Denver: Sage Books, 1962.

Coy, Harold. *Man Comes to America.* Boston: Little, Brown, 1973.

Crosby, Alfred W., Jr. *The Columbian Exchange: Biological and Cultural Consequences of 1492.* Westport, Connecticut: Greenwood Publishing Co., 1972.

Dale, Edward Everett. *The Indians of the Southwest: A Century of Development under the United States.* Norman: University of Oklahoma Press, 1949.

Daniels, Helen Sloan. *The Ute Indians of Southwestern Colorado.* Durango, Colorado: Durango Public Library Museum Project, 1941.

Debo, Angie. *A History of the Indians of the United States.* Norman: University of Oklahoma Press, 1970.

Delaney, Robert W. *The Southern Ute People.* Phoenix, Arizona: Indian Tribal Series, 1974.

Downs, James F. *The Navajo.* New York: Holt, Rinehart & Winston, 1972.

Dozier, Edward P. *The Pueblo Indians of North America.* New York: Holt, Rinehart & Winston, 1970.

Emmitt, Robert. *The Last War Trail: The Utes and the Settlement of Colorado.* Norman: University of Oklahoma Press, 1954.

Erdoes, Richard. *The Sun Dance People.* New York: Alfred A. Knopf, 1972.

Forbes, Jack D. *Apache, Navaho, and Spaniard.* Norman: University of Oklahoma Press, 1960.

Fuchs, Estelle and Robert J. Havighurst. *To Live on This Earth: American Indian Education.* New York: Doubleday, 1972.

Fynn, Arthur John. *The American Indian as a Product of Environment, With Special Reference to the Pueblos.* Boston: Little, Brown, 1907.

------. "The Colorado Indians." *History of Colorado.* Vol. 1. Edited by James H. Baker. State Historical and Natural History Society of Colorado. Denver: Linderman, 1927.

------. *North America in Days of Discovery.* Boston: Richard G. Badger, 1923.

Gilbreath, Kent. *Red Capitalism: An Analysis of the Navajo Economy.* Norman: University of Oklahoma Press, 1973.

Grimm, William C. *Indian Harvests.* New York: McGraw-Hill, 1973.

Grinnell, George Bird. *By Cheyenne Campfires.* New Haven: Yale University Press, 1926.

------. *The Cheyenne Indians: Their History and Ways of Life.* 2 vols. New Haven: Yale University Press, 1924.

Gunnerson, Dolores A. *The Jicarilla Apaches: A Study in Survival.* DeKalb, Illinois: Northern Illinois University Press, 1974.

Hafen, LeRoy R. and Ann W. Hafen, eds. *Relations with the Indians of the Plains, 1857-1861.* Glendale, California: Arthur H. Clark, 1959.

------. *The Colorado Story: A History of Your State and Mine.* Denver: Old West Publishing Co., 1953.

Hafen, LeRoy R. *The Indians of Colorado.* Denver: State Historical Society of Colorado, 1952.

Hart, Gerald T., Leroy R. Hafen, and Anne M. Smith. *Ute Indians II.* Commission Findings: Indian Claims Commission. New York: Garland Publishing, Inc., 1974.

Hassrick, Royal B. *The Sioux: Life and Customs of A Warrior Society.* Norman: University of Oklahoma Press, 1964.

Henry, Jeannette, ed. *The American Indian Reader: Education.* San Francisco: Indian Historian Press, 1972.

Hoebel, E. Adamson. *The Cheyennes: Indians of the Great Plains.* New York: Holt, Rinehart & Winston, 1960.

Howbert, Irving. *The Indians of the Pike's Peak Region.* New York: Knickerbocker Press, 1914.

Hurdy, John Major. *American Indian Religions.* Los Angeles: Sherbourne Press, 1970.

Hurst, C. T. *Colorado's Old-timers: The Indians Back to 25,000 Years Ago.* Gunnison: Colorado Archaeological Society, 1946.

Hyde, George E. *Indians of the High Plains, From the Prehistoric Period to the Coming of Europeans.* Norman: University of Oklahoma Press, 1959.

———. *Life of George Bent.* Norman: University of Oklahoma Press, 1968.

———. *Pawnee Indians.* Denver: University of Denver Press, 1951.

Iacopi, Robert L., Bernard L. Fontana and Charles Jones, eds. *Look To the Mountain Top.* San Jose, California: H. M. Gousha (Times Mirror), 1972.

Jackson, Helen Hunt. *A Century of Dishonor: A Sketch of the United States Government's Dealings with Some of the Indian Tribes.* New York: Harper & Bros., 1881.

Jefferson, James, Robert W. Delaney & Gregory C. Thompson. *The Southern Utes: A Tribal History.* Ignacio, Colorado: Southern Ute Tribe, 1972.

Jorgensen, Joseph G. *The Sun Dance Religion: Power for the Powerless.* Chicago: University of Chicago Press, 1972.

Josephy, Alvin M. *The Indian Heritage of America.* New York: Alfred A. Knopf, 1970.

Kenner, Charles L. *A History of New Mexican-Plains Indian Relations.* Norman: University of Oklahoma Press, 1969.

Kidder, Alfred Vincent. *An Introduction to the Study of Southwestern Archaeology.* New Haven, Connecticut: Yale University (1924), 1962.

Kluckhohn, Clyde and Dorothea Leighton. *The Navaho.* Garden City, New York: Doubleday, 1962.

Lauber, Patricia. *Who Discovered America?* New York: Random House, 1970.

Laubin, Reginald and Gladys Laubin. *The Indian Tipi: Its History, Construction and Use.* Norman: University of Oklahoma Press, 1957.

Lavender, David. *Bent's Fort.* Garden City, New York: Doubleday, 1954.

———. *The Big Divide.* Garden City, New York: Doubleday, 1948.

Linton, Ralph, ed. *Acculturation in Seven American Indian Tribes.* New York: D. Appleton-Century Co., 1940.

Loh, Jules. *Lords of the Earth: A History of the Navajo Indians.* New York: Crowell-Collier, 1971.

Loram, C. T. and T. F. McIlwraith. *The North American Indian Today.* Toronto: University of Toronto Press, 1943.

Lowie, Robert H. *Indians of the Plains.* New York: McGraw-Hill, 1954.

Lyman, June and Norman Denver, comps. *Ute People: An Historical Study.* Edited by Floyd A. O'Neil and John D. Sylvester. Salt Lake City: University of Utah, 1970.

MacGowan, Kenneth. *Early Man in the New World.* New York: Macmillan, 1953.

McGregor, John C. *Southwestern Archaeology.* 2nd ed. Urbana, Ill.: University of Illinois, 1965.

McMechan, Edgar C. "The Indians." Chap. 3 of LeRoy Reuben Hafen. *A Narrative History of the Centennial State.* New York: Lewis Historical Publishing Co., 1948.

MacNeish, Richard S., ed. *Early Man in America.* San Francisco: W. H. Freeman, 1973.

Mails, Thomas E. *The Mystic Warriors of the Plains.* Garden City, New York: Doubleday, 1972.

Mardock, Robert Winston. *The Reformers and the American Indian.* Columbia, Mo.: University of Missouri Press, 1971.

Mayhall, Mildred P. *The Kiowas.* Norman: University of Oklahoma Press, 1962.

Meriam, Lewis. *Problems of Indian Administration.* Baltimore: Johns Hopkins, 1928.

Momaday, N. Scott. *The Way to Rainy Mountain.* Albuquerque, New Mexico: University of New Mexico Press, 1969.

Morey, Sylvester M. *Can the Red Man Help the White Man? Report of a Denver Conference with American Indian Elders.* New York: G. Church, 1970.

———, and Olivia L. Gilliam, eds. *Respect for Life: The Traditional Upbringing of American Indian Children.* Garden City, New York: Waldorf Press, 1974.

Nichols, Roger L. and George R. Adams, eds. *The American Indian: Past and Present.* Waltham, Mass.: Xerox College Publishing, 1971.

Nordenskioeld, G. *The Cliff Dwellers of the Mesa Verde, Southwestern Colorado: Their Pottery and Implements.* Stockholm: P. A. Norstedt & Soener, 1893. (Reprinted New York: A.M.S. Press, 1973.)

Nye, Wilbur Sturtevant. *Bad Medicine and Good: Tales of the Kiowas.* Norman: University of Oklahoma Press, 1962.

Olden, Sarah Emilia. *Shoshone Folk Lore.* Milwaukee: Morehouse, 1923.

Opler, Morris Edward. *Myths and Tales of the Jicarilla Apache Indians.* New York: American Folk-Lore Society, 1938.

Parkhill, Forbes. *The Last of the Indian Wars.* New York: Collier Books, 1961.

Parkman, Francis. *The Oregon Trail.* New York: New American Library, 1950.

Parsons, Elsie Clews. *Kiowa Tales.* New York: American Folk-Lore Society, 1929.

Peckham, Howard and Charles Gibson, eds. *Attitudes of Colonial Powers toward the American Indian.* Salt Lake City: University of Utah Press, 1969.

Pike, Donald G. and David Muench. *Anasazi: Ancient People of the Rock.* Palo Alto, California: American West, 1974.

Powell, Peter J. *Sweet Medicine: The Continuing Role of the Sacred Arrows, the Sun Dance, and the Sacred Buffalo Hat in Northern Cheyenne History.* 2 vols. Norman: University of Oklahoma Press, 1969.

Prucha, Francis Paul, ed. *Americanizing the American Indians: Writings by the "Friends of the Indian" 1880–1900.* Cambridge, Mass.: Harvard University Press, 1973.

Renaud, Etienne Bernardeau. "The Indians of Colorado." Reprinted from Henderson, Junius, E. B. Renaud, Colin B. Goodykoontz, et. al. *Colorado: Short Studies of its Past and Present.* Boulder: University of Colorado Press, 1927.

Richardson, Albert D. *Beyond the Mississippi.* Hartford, Conn.: American Publishing Co., 1867.

Richardson, Rupert Norval. *The Comanche Barrier to South Plains Settlement.* Glendale, California: Arthur H. Clark, 1933.

Rockwell, Wilson. *The Utes: A Forgotten People.* Denver: Sage Books, 1956.

Sandoz, Mari. *Cheyenne Autumn.* New York: McGraw-Hill, 1953.

Scully, Virginia. *A Treasury of American Indian Herbs.* New York: Crown Publishers, 1970.

Sellards, E. H. *Early Man in America.* Austin: University of Texas, 1952.

Southern Ute Tribe. *Progress: A Report by the Southern Ute Tribe.* Ignacio, Colorado: Southern Ute Tribe, 1958.

——. *Progress and the Future.* Dallas, Texas: Taylor Publishing Co., 1966.

——. *Rehabilitation Plan of the Southern Ute Tribe.* Ignacio, Colorado: N.P., 1954.

——. *Where We Stand: A Report by the Southern Ute Tribe.* Ignacio, Colorado: N.P., 1960.

Spicer, Edward H. *Cycles of Conquest: The Impact of Spain, Mexico and the United States on the Indians of the Southwest, 1533-1960.* Tucson: University of Arizona Press, 1962.

Sprague, Marshall. *Massacre: The Tragedy at White River.* Boston: Little, Brown, 1957. 2nd edition. New York: Ballantine, 1972.

Stands in Timber, John and Margot Liberty. *Cheyenne Memories.* New Haven: Yale University Press, 1967.

Steiner, Stan. *The New Indians.* New York: Harper & Row, 1968.

Steward, Julian H. *Ute Indians I.* New York: Garland Publishing, 1974.

Stirling, Matthew W. *Indians of the Americas.* Washington, D. C.: National Geographic Society, 1955.

Stuart, George E. and Gene S. Stuart. *Discovering Man's Past in the Americas.* Washington, D. C.: National Geographic Society (1969), 1973.

Szasz, Margaret. *Education and the American Indian: The Road to Self-Determination, 1928-1973.* Albuquerque: University of New Mexico Press, 1974.

Taylor, Theodore W. *The States and Their Indian Citizens* USDI BIA, 1972. Washington: GPO, 1972.

Terrell, John Upton. *Apache Chronicle.* New York: World, 1972.

——. *The Navajos: The Past and Present of a Great People.* New York: Weybright & Talley, 1970.

Trenholm, Virginia C. *The Arapahoes, Our People.* Norman: University of Oklahoma Press, 1970.

——, and Maurine Carley. *The Shoshonis: Sentinels of the Rockies.* Norman: University of Oklahoma Press, 1964.

Tyler, Daniel, ed. *Western American History in the Seventies.* Ft. Collins, Colorado: Robinson Press, 1973.

Tyler, S. Lyman. *A History of Indian Policy.* Washington, D.C.: U.S. Dept. of the Interior, Bureau of Indian Affairs, 1973.

Ubbelohde, Carl, Maxine Benson & Duane A. Smith. *A Colorado History.* 3rd Edition. Boulder, Colorado: Pruett, 1972.

Underhill, Ruth Murray. *The Navajos.* Norman: University of Oklahoma Press, 1956.

——. *Red Man's America.* Chicago: University of Chicago Press, 1953.

——. *Red Man's Religion.* Chicago: University of Chicago Press, 1965.

U.S. Court of Claims. *The Confederated Bands of Ute Indians vs. the United States of America. Plaintiff's Proposed Findings of Fact under Rule 39(a),* 2 vols. Ernest L. Wilkinson, Attorney of Record. U.S. Court of Claims, No. 45585.

USDI. *Annual Reports of the Department of the Interior. 1906. Indian Affairs. "Reports Concerning Indians in Colorado," pp. 210-213 (Fort Lewis School, Grand Junction School, Southern Ute Agency).* Washington, D. C.: GPO, 1907.

USDI. *Fifty-third Annual Report of the Board of Indian Commissioners to the Secretary of the Interior for the Fiscal Year Ended June 30, 1922. "Ute Mountain Indian Agency, Colorado," pp. 16-17.* Washington, D. C.: GPO, 1922.

USDI. *Annual Report of the Board of Indian Commissioners to the Secretary of the Interior for the Fiscal Year Ended June 30, 1932. G. E. E. Lindquist, "Consolidated Ute Indian Agency, Colorado," pp. 24-25.* Washington, D. C.: GPO, 1932.

USDI Office of Indian Affairs. *Constitution and By-laws of the Ute Mountain Tribe of the Ute Mountain Reservation, Colorado, New Mexico, Utah. Approved June 6, 1940.* Ignacio, Colorado: Ignacio Chieftain (after 1950).

Utley, Robert M. *Frontier Regulars: The United States Army and the Indian, 1866-1890.* New York: Macmillan, 1973.

——. *Frontiersmen in Blue: The United States Army and the Indian, 1848-1865.* New York: Macmillan, 1967.

Van Roekel, Gertrude B. *Jicarilla Apaches.* San Antonio, Texas: Naylor, 1971.

Vestal, Paul A. and Richard Evans Schultes. *The Economic Botany of the Kiowa Indians as It Relates to the History of the Tribe.* Cambridge, Mass.: Botanical Museum, 1939.

Vogel, Virgil J. *American Indian Medicine.* Norman: University of Oklahoma Press, 1970.

Waddell, Jack O. and Michael Watson, eds. *The American Indian in Urban Society.* Boston: Little, Brown, 1971.

Walker, Deward E., Jr. *The Emergent Native Americans: A Reader in Contact Culture.* Boston: Little, Brown, 1971.

Wallace, Ernest and E. Adamson Hoebel. *The Comanches: Lords of the South Plains.* Norman: University of Oklahoma Press, 1952.

Watson, Don. *Indians of the Mesa Verde.* Mesa Verde National Park, Colo.: Mesa Verde Museum Association, 1961.

Wax, Murray L. *Indian Americans: Unity and Diversity.* Englewood Cliffs, New Jersey: Prentice-Hall, 1971.

Weaver, Thomas, ed. *Indians of Arizona: A Contemporary Perspective.* Tucson, Arizona: University of Arizona Press, 1974.

Wedel, Waldo R. *Prehistoric Man on the Great Plains.* Norman: University of Oklahoma Press, 1961.

Will, George F. and George E. Hyde. *Corn among the Indians of the Upper Missouri.* Lincoln, Nebraska: University of Nebraska Press, 1917.

Willey, Gordon R. *An Introduction to American Archaeology.* Vol. 1: *North and Middle America.* Englewood Cliffs, New Jersey: Prentice-Hall, 1966.

Wilmsen, Edwin N. *Lindenmeier: A Pleistocene Hunting Society.* New York: Harper & Row, 1974.

Wilson, H. Clyde. *Jicarilla Apache Political and Economic Structures.* Berkeley, California: University of California Press, 1964.

Wormington, Hannah Marie. "When Did Man Come to North America?" in *Ancient Hunters of the Far West.* Edited by James S. Copley. San Diego, California: Union-Tribune, 1966.

Articles:

Anderson, Harry H. "Stand at the Arikaree." *Colorado Magazine,* 41 (1964), 336–42.

Bada, Jeffray L., Roy A. Schroeder and George F. Carter. "New Evidence for the Antiquity of Man in North America Deduced from Aspartic Acid Racemization." *Science,* 184 (May 17, 1974), 791–93.

Berkhofer, Robert J., Jr. "The Political Context of a New Indian History." *Pacific Historical Review,* 40 (1971), 357–82.

Buck, Charles. "The Troubles of the Indians." *Denver Field and Farm,* August 1914.

Buckles, William G. "Archaeology in Colorado: Historic Tribes." *Southwestern Lore,* 34 (1968), 53–67.

Carey, Raymond G. "The Puzzle of Sand Creek." *Colorado Magazine,* 41 (1964), 279–298.

Cordell, Linda S. and Mindy H. Halpern. "Anasazi Nucleation for Defense: Reasons to Doubt an Obvious Solution." *Rocky Mountain Social Science Journal,* 12 (April, 1975), 41–48.

Dick, Herbert W. "The Status of Colorado Archaeology, with a Bibliographic Guide." *Southwestern Lore,* 18 (March, 1953), 53–77.

Eggan, Fred. "From History to Myth: A Hopi Example." *Studies in Southwestern Ethnolinguistics: Meaning and History in the Languages of the American Southwest.* Edited by Del H. Hymes and William E. Bittle. The Hague: Mouton, 1967.

Elisha, M. J. "The Present Status of Basketmaker II and III Sites in Colorado." *Southwestern Lore,* 34 (1968), 33–47.

Emmitt, Robert P. "Indians in Colorado." *Denver Westerners' Roundup,* 31 (January, 1975), 3–11.

Filipiak, Jack D. "The Battle of Summit Springs." *Colorado Magazine,* 41 (1964), 343–54.

Forbes, Jack D. "The Appearance of the Mounted Indian in Northern Mexico and the Southwest, to 1680." *Southwestern Journal of Anthropology,* 15 (1959), 189–212.

Gunnerson, Dolores A. "The Southern Athabascans: Their Arrival in the Southwest." *El Palacio,* 6 (November-December, 1956), 347–65.

Haug, James D. "[The Archaeology of Colorado: Part I], Prehistoric Eastern Colorado, 10,000 B.C. to 1 A.D." *Southwestern Lore,* 34 (June, 1968), 1–10.

Heath, G. Louis. "The Life and Education of the American Indian." *Illinois Quarterly,* 33 (1971), 16–38.

123

Hoffmeister, Harold. "The Consolidated Ute Indian Reservation." *Geographical Review,* 35 (1945), 601-23.

Hughes, J. Donald. "The De-racialization of Historical Atlases: A Modest Proposal." *Indian Historian,* 7 (1974), 55-57.

Jacobs, Wilbur R. "Native American History: How It Illuminates Our Past." *American Historical Review,* 80 (June, 1975), 595-609.

Jennings, Calvin H. "The Paleo-Indian and Archaic Stages in Western Colorado." *Southwestern Lore,* 34 (1968), 11-20.

Lecompte, Janet. "Sand Creek." *Colorado Magazine,* 41 (1964), 314-35.

Marquardt, Cynthia. "Basic Data on Early Sites in Colorado and Adjacent Regions." *Southwestern Lore,* 34 (1968), 21-30.

Miller, Ross V. "Shawsheen: The Heroine of the Meeker Massacre." *The Brand Book (The Westerners),* March, 1951.

Newcomb, W. W., Jr. "A re-examination of the Causes of Plains Warfare." *American Anthropologist,* 52 (1950), 317-30.

Opler, Morris Edward. "A Summary of Jicarilla Apache Culture." *American Anthropologist,* 38 (1936), 202-22.

Scher, Zeke. "Colorado's Hope for the Red Man." *Denver Post, Empire,* June 28, 1970, 8-12.

Schroeder, Albert H. "A Brief History of the Southern Utes." *Southwestern Lore,* 30 (October 1954), 53-80.

Sievers, Michael A. "Sands of Sand Creek Historiography." *Colorado Magazine,* 49 (1972), 116-42.

Stacher, S. F. "The Indians of the Ute Mountain Reservation, 1906-9." *Colorado Magazine,* 26 (1949), 52-61.

Stewart, Omer C. "Ute Indians: Before and After White Contact." *Utah Historical Quarterly,* 34 (1966), 38-61.

Tyler, S. Lyman. "The Spaniard and the Ute." *Utah Historical Quarterly,* 22 (October 1954), 343-61.

———. "The Yuta Indians Before 1680." *Western Humanities Review,* 5 (Spring, 1951), 153-63.

Unrau, William E. "A Prelude to War." *Colorado Magazine,* 41 (1964), 299-313.

Washburn, Wilcomb. "The Writing of American Indian History: A Status Report." *Pacific Historical Review,* 40 (1971), 261-81.

Wedel, Waldo R. "Some Aspects of Human Ecology in the Central Plains." *American Anthropologist,* 55 (1953), 499-514.

Theses and Dissertations:

Baker, Augusta. "The Ute Indians." Unpublished M.A. thesis, University of Denver, 1926.

Cornell, Lois Adelaide. "The Jicarilla Apaches: Their History, Customs and Present Status." Unpublished M.A. thesis, University of Colorado, 1927.

Fant, Olna Hudler. "A Biographical and Critical Study of Helen Hunt Jackson." Unpublished M.A. thesis, University of Denver, 1931.

Hoyt, Milton. "Development of Education among the Southern Utes." Unpublished Ed.D. thesis, University of Colorado, n.d.

Kennedy, Lawrence Michael. "The Colorado Press and the Red Men: Local Opinion about Indian Affairs, 1859-1870." Unpublished M.A. thesis, University of Denver, 1967.

Swadesh, Frances Leon. "The Southern Utes and their Neighbors, 1877-1926: An Ethnohistorical Study of Multiple Interaction in Contact-Induced Cultural Change." Unpublished M.A. thesis, University of Colorado, 1962.

Tiller, Veronica Velarde. "Recent History of the Jicarilla Apache Tribe, 1870-1934." Unpublished M.A. thesis, University of New Mexico, 1973.

Reports and Serials:

Breternitz, David A., ed. *Archaeological Excavations in Dinosaur National Monument, Colorado-Utah, 1964-1965.* University of Colorado Studies, Series in Anthropology, No. 17. Boulder, Colorado: University of Colorado Press, August, 1970.

Carlson, Roy L. *Basket Maker III Sites near Durango, Colorado.* University of Colorado Studies, Series in Anthropology, No. 8, The Earl Morris Papers, No. 1. Boulder, Colorado: University of Colorado Press, June, 1963.

Densmore, Frances. *Cheyenne and Arapahoe Music.* Southwest Museum Papers, No. 10. Los Angeles: n.p., May, 1936.

Dick, Herbert W. *Bat Cave.* The School of American Research, Monograph No. 27. Santa Fe, New Mexico: n.p., 1965.

Ditert, Alfred E., Jr., Jim J. Hester and Frank W. Eddy. *An Archaeological Survey of the Navajo Reservoir District, Northwestern New Mexico.* Monographs of the School of American Research and the Museum of New Mexico, No. 23. Santa Fe, New Mexico: n.p., 1961.

Dorsey, George A. *The Arapaho Sun Dance: The Ceremony of the Offerings Lodge.* Fieldiana: Anthropology, Publication 75, Anthropological Series, Vol. 4. Chicago: Natural History Museum, June, 1903.

—— and Alfred L. Kroeber. *Traditions of the Arapaho.* Fieldiana: Anthropology, Publication 81, Anthropological Series, Vol. 5. Chicago: Natural History Museum, October, 1903.

Douglas, Frederic H. *The Ute Indians.* Denver Art Museum, Leaflet Series, No. 10, pp. 1-4.

Fay, George E. *Land Cessions In Utah and Colorado by the Ute Indians, 1861-1899.* Museum of Anthropology, Miscellaneous Series, No. 13. Fort Collins, Colorado: University of Northern Colorado Press, July, 1970.

Goddard, Pliny Earle. *Jicarilla Apache Texts.* Anthropological Papers of the American Museum of Natural History, Vol. 8. New York: n.p., 1911.

Gunnerson, James H. *The Fremont Culture: A Study in Culture Dynamics on the Northern Anasazi Frontier.* Papers of the Peabody Museum of Archaeology and Ethnology, Vol. 59, No. 2. Cambridge, Mass.: Harvard University Press, 1969.

Jablow, Joseph. *The Cheyenne in Plains Indian Trade Relations 1795-1840.* Monographs of the American Ethnological Society, No. 19. New York: J. J. Augustin, 1950.

Kroeber, Alfred L. *The Arapaho*. Bulletin of the American Museum of Natural History, Vol. 18, 1902.

——. "Symbolism of the Arapaho Indians." Bulletin of the American Museum of Natural History, Vol. 13, pp. 69–89, 1900.

Lauber, Almon Wheeler. *Indian Slavery in Colonial Times within the Present Limits of the United States*. Studies in History, Economics and Public Law, Columbia University, Vol. 54, No. 3, Whole Number 134. New York: Columbia University, 1913.

Liberty, Margot. *Fights with the Shoshone, 1855–1870: A Northern Cheyenne Indian Narrative*. Occasional Papers, Montana State University, No. 2. Missoula: Montana State University Press, Feb. 1961.

Lowie, Robert H. *Dances and Societies of the Plains Shoshone*. American Museum of Natural History Anthropological Papers, Vol. 11, Part 10. New York, 1915.

Martin, Paul S. *Modified Basket Maker Sites, Ackmen-Lowry Area, Southwestern Colorado, 1938*. Field Museum of Natural History Anthropological Series, Vol. 23, No. 3 (Publication 444). Chicago, June, 1939.

Morss, Noel. *The Ancient Culture of the Fremont River in Utah*. Peabody Museum of American Archaeology and Ethnology, Harvard University, Papers, Vol. 12, No. 3. Cambridge, Mass.: Harvard University Press.

Miller, Wick R., compiler. *Newe Natekwinappeh: Shoshoni Stories and Dictionary*. University of Utah Anthropological Papers, No. 94. Salt Lake City: University of Utah Press, 1972.

O'Bryan, Deric. *Excavations in Mesa Verde National Park, 1947–1948*. Gila Pueblo, Medallion Papers, No. 39. Globe, Arizona, June, 1950.

Opler, Morris Edward. *Childhood and Youth in Jicarilla Apache Society*. Southwest Museum, Publications of the Frederick Webb Hodge Anniversary Publication Fund, Vol. 5. Los Angeles, 1946.

Shimkin, D. B. *Childhood and Development among the Wind River Shoshone*. Anthropological Records, Vol. 5, No. 5. Berkeley: University of California Press, 1947.

——. *Wind River Shoshone Ethnogeography*. Anthropological Records, Vol. 5, No. 4. Berkeley: University of California Press, 1947.

Stevens, David Walter. *Capital as a Determinant of Economic Growth: Allocation in a Tri-Ethnic Community*. Research Report No. 48, Tri-Ethnic Research Project. Boulder: University of Colorado, 1965.

Stewart, Omer C. *Ethnohistorical Bibliography of the Ute Indians of Colorado*. University of Colorado Studies, Series in Anthropology No. 18. Boulder: University of Colorado Press, 1971.

——. *Ute Peyotism: A Study of A Cultural Complex*. University of Colorado, Series in Anthropology, No. 1, 1948. Boulder: University of Colorado Press, September 1948.

Swanson, Earl H., ed. *Utaztekan Prehistory*. Idaho State University Museum, Occasional Papers, No. 22, 1968.

Tyler, S. Lyman. *The Ute People: A Bibliographical Checklist*. Provo, Utah: Brigham Young University, 1964.

Wissler, Clark, ed. *Sun Dance of the Plains Indian.* American Museum of Natural History, Anthropological Papers, Vol. 16, 1921.

Wormington, Hannah Marie. *Ancient Man In North America.* Denver Museum of Natural History, Popular Series No. 4, Fourth Edition, 1957.

——. *Prehistoric Indians of the Southwest.* Denver Museum of Natural History, Popular Series No. 7, Third Edition, 1956.

Zingg, Robert Mowry. *A Reconstruction of Uto-Aztekan History.* Chicago: University of Chicago Libraries, 1937.

Index

66, 68, 84; races, 93
Hosa, Chief (Little Raven), 57
hospitality, 21, 41
hospitals, 89, 98-99
hostiles, 59
hotel, 93
housing, 2, 81, 90, 98, 100, 103-105, 108. *See also* shelter
Hunt, Alexander Cameron, 62
Hunter Act, 71
hunters, commercial, 62
hunting, 2-3, 7, 10-14, 20-21, 24, 27-28, 30, *31,* 33, 36, 39, 41, 61, 66, 82, 84; rights, 111; territories, 27
Hunting Tradition, *72*

Ice Age, 7, 10
Idaho, 33
Ignacio, Colorado, 1, 67, *76-77,* 80, 88-89, 93-94, 99, 101, 108
Ignacio, Ute chief, 71, 79, 97
Ignacio public school, 89
Illinois, 52
Inca, 42
Indian, definition, 3-4
Indiana, 52
Indian Claims Act, 111
Indian desks, 107
Indianism, 91
Indian Reorganization Act, 96-97
Indian Rights Association, 70-71, 90, 93-95
Indians, policy towards the United States, 54
Indian Territory, 52, 66
infant care, 16
infant mortality, 89
inheritance, 83
Inunaina, 36
Irish, 6, 39
irrigation, 16, 83, 98
Italians, 2, 6, 39

Jack, 62, 68
jackrabbits, 27
Jackson, Andrew, 52-53
Jackson, Helen Maria Hunt, 70
Jackson, William H., *28*

Japanese, 39, 103
Jemez, 44
jerky, 23
jet inlay, 18
Jicarilla, 30
Jicarilla. *See* Apaches, Jicarilla
Johnson, 68
Johnson, Andrew, 62
Johnson-O'Malley Act, 101
Julesburg, 61, *76*
juniper bark, 14

kachinas, 15, *15,* 44
Kaneache, 62, 103
Kansas, 23, 33, 38, 44-45, 52-53, 56, 61, 67
Kearny, Stephen Watts, 47
Kent, Bonny, *96*
Kershaw, J. W., 94
King of Spain, 43
Kiowa, 21, 34-35, 37, 56, 61, *75;* language, 34
Kiowa-Apache, 21, 33-35, 61
Kit Carson, Colorado, 12, *72*
kivas, 16-17, 19-20; great, 16, 19
knives, 42, 48
Korea, 103

La Junta, 46
Lakota, 38. *See also* Sioux
land, 4, 6, 42-43, 47-48, 51-53, 56-58, 61-62, 65, 68, 70-71, 79, 82-84, 88, 95-98, 103, 109, 111, 114; Indian school, 109; public, 51, 53; surplus, 70, 97. *See also* allotments
land grants, Mexican, 47
languages, Indian, 3, 5, 21, 23, 85, 95, 103. *See also* sign language
La Plata County, 101
La Plata River, 69
La Veta Pass, 54
law enforcement, 25, 81, 97, 106
lawyers, 79, 111
learning center, 101
leatherwork, 2, 23-24, 28, 30, 91
Left Hand, 57
legal counsel, 111

pipe, sacred, 26, 35, *37*
pipes, 15
pithouses, 14, 16, 20
plains, 2, 7, 12–13, 21, 23–24, 27, 29–30, 33, 36–37, 41, 43, 56, 61, 110
Plains Archaic tradition, 13
Plains cultural area, 22, 26, 33–39, 108
Plains Indians, 22–29, 34–39, 44, 46, 57, 59–62, 108
planting, 13–14, 41. *See also* agriculture
plants, 2, 12, 114; cultivated, 13; curative, 15, 89; food, 27; spirits, 29; wild, 13, 20, *23*, 30
plateau, 12, 33
plaza, 19
pluralism, 95
poetry, 2, 33
police, Indian or tribal, 25, 81, 97
political action, Indian, 112–13
Polk Narraguinnep, 94
pollution, 114
Ponca, 38
popcorn, 13
Pope, 44
population, Indian, 1, 89–90, 105
porcupine quills, 24
Posey, 94
pottery, 13–14, 17–20, 24, 28, 30, 32, 42, 99
poverty, 95
power, 25–26, 31, 92
pow-wows, *102, 106, 107–108*
prayers, 26, *37*, 91–92
prayer sticks, 15
prejudice, anti-Indian, 89
Presbyterians, 88, 93
priests, Catholic, 42, 93
printing, *87*
private enterprise, 98
projectile points, 9, 11, 13–14
pronghorn antelope. *See* antelope
Protestants, 93
public relations, 97, 113
Pueblo, Colorado, 45–46, 55, *76*

Pueblo Indians, 3, 16–22, 28–30, 32, 34, 41–45, 49, *72–75*, 80, 93, 95; languages, 16
Pueblo Revolt, 44
pumpkins, 13
Purgatoire River, 57

Querechos, 41
quillwork, 2, 24
Quinkent, 115 n. 12
Quiziachigiate, 54

rabbits, 10, 12, 20, 27–28
race, relay, 30
radio, 22
radiocarbon dating, 10–11
raids, 31, 34, 38, 44, 56, 59, 61
railroads, 54, 61, 69–70
Ralston, Lewis, 53
Ramona, 70
ranches, 47, 67
rations, 54, 56, 58, 82
Raton, 46
Raton Pass, 47
rattles, 92
recreation, 107
Red Cap, 90
Red Dog, *65*
Red Men, 9
Redrock, 79
reformers, 66, 70–71, 94
religion, 2, 5, 15, 18, 25–26, 29–31, 35–36, 43–44, 64–65, 91–93, 95, 108
religious freedom, 92–93, 95
relocation, 104
removal, Indian, 51–72, 94
reptiles, 13
reservations, 1, 5, 7, 58, 61, 70, 82, 103–105; Arapaho, 57, *76;* Cheyenne, 57, *76;* Cheyenne River Sioux, 90; Delaware, 52; Jicarilla Apache, 67, *77;* Kiowa, 35; Navajo, 32, *77*, 88, 104; Northern Cheyenne, 67; Southern Ute, 71–72, *77*, 79–102; Uintah-Ouray, *77*, 90; Ute (Colorado), 62–69, 71, *76–77*, 79–102; Ute (Utah), 69, 71, *77*, 94; Ute Mountain, 71, *77*, 79–102

dians, 58
White Buffalo Council, 106-107, *106*
White River, 63-64, 67-68, *76-77*
White River Agency, 64, 67-68, *76*
White River Utes, 62, 64, 67-69, 90
Wichita, 38
Wichita Mountains, 35
Wind River, 33
Winnebago, 38, 95
Wisconsin, 38
Wisconsin glaciation, 10
wolves, 10, 58
women, status of, 14, 24-25, 29-30, 46-47, 98
wood, 23
wood carving, 24
Woodland culture, 13, 35, *72*
wool, 17, 32
World War: First, 82; Second, 97, 103
Wounded Knee: First Incident, 91; Second Incident, 113
Wynkoop, Edward W., 60
Wyoming, 33-35, 39, 56, 61, 90

Yamparika, 34
Yampa River, 27, 33, *72, 76-77*
Yampa root, *23,* 27, 34
Yampa Utes, 27, *73*
Yellowstone National Park, 62
Yellowstone River, 33-34
Yellow Wolf, 48
Yellow Woman, 48
Yohovits, 29
youth camp, 101
yucca, 14, 27

Zuni, 16

The University of Denver
Department of History
Colorado Ethnic History Series

American Indians of Colorado is the first of a series of books devoted to a hitherto-neglected aspect of the history of the West—those groups (some of which we call "minorities") who formed the backbone of life, labor, and civilization in Colorado. The story is a long one—the Spanish came through here in 1776, the Indians were here long before them. French names dot the landscape, reminders of early explorers and trappers.

Accounts of these various peoples stop, unfortunately, with the coming of the twentieth century, or with the first World War. Authors in this series will give us the whole picture, beginning with the first appearance of these groups and take the story right down to the present, on the farm, in the mining and resort areas, and in the towns and cities of our day.

Other books in this series, which will appear at regular intervals, include:

Black Americans

The English

The Welsh

The Scots

The Irish

The German-Speaking
  Peoples

The Greeks

The Slavs

The Spanish-Surnamed

The Canadians

The Chinese

The Japanese

The Dutch

The Italians

The Scandinavians (in separate studies):

  The Swedes, the Norwegians, the Danes

The Jews

Finally, there will be **The People of Colorado** by Allen D. Breck and Lyle W. Dorsett of the University of Denver. Here will be a discussion of the principles by which ethnic history must be written and will focus on the history of those groups to which a whole monograph cannot be given.

For further information about the series write:

Department of History
The University of Denver
Denver, Colorado 80210

or

Pruett Publishing Company
2928 Pearl Street
Boulder, Colorado 80301